Beyond Influencer Marketing

Create Connections with Influential People to Build Authority, Grow Your List, and Boost Revenue

CLORIS KYLIE

Beyond Influencer Marketing

Create Connections with Influential People to Build Authority, Grow Your List, and Boost Revenue

Cloris Kylie, MBA Copyright (c) 2018, 2019 by Cloris Kylie LLC

Library of Congress Control Number: 2018900055

ISBN 978-0-9997221-0-7 (Print)

ISBN 978-0-9997221-1-4 (Kindle)

ISBN 978-0-9997221-2-1 (Audiobook)

BONUS: Free membership for readers of *Beyond Influencer Marketing* ($197 value)

Claim your free templates to kickstart your influencer marketing efforts and help you grow your magnificent business…

- Intro email formula to expand your network and get referrals

- Copy-and-paste templates:
  - Podcast pitch
  - TV appearance pitch
  - Guest-post pitch

And much more! Claim your book bonuses now:

www.beyondinfluencermarketing.com/bonuses

What entrepreneurs are saying about Cloris

"Cloris's expertise has helped me better understand my business."

"Cloris knows her stuff. Building on her unique foundation as an engineer and an entrepreneur, Cloris is able to take the complex and break it down into easy-to-understand systems that can be replicated and scaled for business success. Her expertise has helped me better understand my business."

Alain Hunkins
Leadership Development Consultant

"I was blown away by Cloris's over-delivery of high-quality, useful information and instruction that works!"

"Cloris is a great coach and someone I listen to because she knows what she's talking about. I am a bestselling author, but I don't YET have a 'business' other than book sales. And, as usual, I was blown away by Cloris' over-delivery of high-quality, useful information and instruction that works! I began implementing Cloris' instructions immediately—that's how much trust I have in her!"

Greg Kuhn
**Bestselling Author of the *Why Quantum Physicists*
Series, Speaker, and Coach**

"Cloris guides you step by step through what it takes to be successful in an online business."

"Cloris guides you step by step through what it takes to be successful in an online business. If you follow her guidance, you will be able to bypass many of the mistakes I made when I started. She's been there and she knows how it's done and she can teach you how to do it, too."

Michelle Martin Dobbins
Author of *Personal Alchemy* and *Relationship Alchemy*, Blogger, and Online Trainer

"If you want your business to take off, you need to hire Cloris."

"Cloris is the ultimate strategist, knowing exactly what needs to be done first so that I build a truly secure platform on which to grow my business. Not only is she a pleasure to work with, but she also has a special way of getting me to do things I may procrastinate on. She doesn't let anything slide by her, that's for sure. I cannot recommend Cloris enough. If you want to get your business to take off, you need to hire Cloris. You won't regret it!!"

Fiona Bain, MBA
Women's Empowerment Coach

"Cloris is one of the most reliable professionals I know."

"I've been impressed with Cloris's passion for her work, her hardworking nature, and her drive to create only the highest quality coaching and training programs for her clients. Cloris is one of the most reliable professionals I know, and it's a pleasure to recommend her and her services."

Roz Savage
Bestselling Author, World-Renowned Speaker,
and Coach

"Cloris will help you get in front of the right people, in the right way, and in the perfect time."

"Cloris is such a powerful leader. She is authentic, and she provides real value to those that are just starting out, or those that want to take their business to the next level. She will walk you step by step on how to connect to those at the top so you can get your message to those that are waiting for it. If you want to stand out, Cloris will help you get in front of the right people, in the right way, and in the perfect time."

Susan Bradley-Boartfield
Transformational Leader, Coach, and Mentor

Dedication

To my mom. I'm forever blessed and grateful for your unconditional loving support.

To my dad, for your everlasting love and inspiration.

Table of Contents

Introduction

The handwritten letter that changed the course of my life

triple-checked the zip code before dropping the envelope in the mail. "I'm not even sure this will get to him, but I'll take a chance," I thought.

In that letter I mailed to world-renowned author and speaker Dr. Wayne W. Dyer, I said thanks. I yearned to thank him for his message of self-reliance that helped me survive one of the most tumultuous times in my life.

In the letter, I also asked him if it would be possible to thank him in person at an upcoming Hay House Publishers conference I was planning to attend.

As weeks went by, I forgot about the letter, although I continued to seek comfort and peace in Wayne's books. Then, one morning, my heart skipped a beat when I saw a big envelope from Maui with Dr. Wayne W. Dyer as the sender.

In the envelope, I found Wayne's handwritten note with instructions explaining how to connect with him at the conference.

I'll never forget the day we met. "You deserve an extraordinary life," he said. His reassuring words not only gave me strength to continue dealing with my personal troubles, but also sparked an idea: I was going to write a book about my challenge. I was going to help others who, like me, were coping with separation and divorce.

A new path—and new challenges

I wrote my personal development book in three months. The words flowed easily because I was relating what was happening in my life at that exact moment. Wayne became a mentor and a role model. We stayed in touch, and, inspired by his guidance, I attended several conferences for writers.

I learned about the importance of building a "writer's platform," so I started blogging daily. I would gain inspiration from taking walks, reading books, or meeting new people.

I also started a live online radio show, "Magnificent Time," in which I explored self-empowerment. My first radio show episodes were monologues, based on my personal interpretation of self-help books.

I thought the blog and the show would help me bring awareness to my recently published book.

Boy, was I wrong…

I quickly realized that it wasn't easy to gain new readers and listeners. It seemed that I was shouting my message into an empty room.

All of this happened before the Internet boom, when blogging and podcasting were still in their early years. Google's "Blogger" was the tool of choice for many at the time (including me).

I considered buying ads to promote my work, but I was afraid of tapping into my savings. I had been a business owner for years, but I had never felt financially vulnerable because I knew I could count on my husband's paycheck to cover unexpected expenses. Now that I was on my own, I wondered whether I'd be better off getting a "real job" with a steady paycheck and benefits.

However, my inner voice told me to continue pursuing my calling, so I kept my offline business and started looking for ways to grow my new business online.

Without a huge ad budget, I didn't know what else to do to build an audience except for creating content and sharing it on social media.

No matter how much valuable content I created, my audience was growing at a snail's pace. Did anyone care about what I had to say?

The constant sense of working hard and getting paltry results was draining... I had to think of a better and faster way to get my name out.

My aha moment

One day, I listened to a few other radio shows and realized that most of them weren't monologues. Instead, they were interview-based.

Aha! It hadn't occurred to me that having guests would help me spread the word about my show!

Around the same time, I heard about "guest blogging." Brilliant, I thought. Someone with an existing readership would publish my articles. No more struggling for hours on end to attract readers. I was ecstatic!

That's when my perspective on how to build a platform entirely changed.

Confident I had a valuable message and enough talent, I realized I only needed to find others who would help me gain momentum and get over the initial hump.

What happened next

Connecting with that first group of influencers (podcast guests and bloggers) opened the door to new connections and new mentors. They taught me about specialized training programs that would help my business grow. After an intensive learning phase, I felt as though I had gone through a second MBA program in digital marketing.

Opportunities to collaborate with my connections and to be featured on their platforms started to appear.

One opportunity led to the next, and to the next...

I had entered a whole new world, and I loved it.

Fast-forward a few years, and here I am, featured on blogs with millions of readers, podcasts with millions of followers, virtual summits with thousands of attendees, local events with hundreds of entrepreneurs, and YouTube and television shows with millions of viewers.

Now, instead of slaving over the computer creating content and programs no one seemed to care about, I focus my efforts on serving audiences consisting of my ideal clients.

Now, I don't depend on Facebook or any other advertising platform to attract new clients and grow my business.

Now, the fear and constant sense of being overwhelmed that used to keep me awake at night have been replaced with confidence and ease. I feel blessed to experience the satisfaction of making a difference in the lives of entrepreneurs all over the world.

Now, when I open my eyes in the morning, I can't wait to get up and continue doing what I love.

Why "Beyond" Influencer Marketing? Beyond What?

Influencer marketing is one of the latest marketing trends, but for this strategy to truly work for you over the long term, you need to see it as more than a trend.

Instead of conceptualizing it as a one-time deal when someone with an audience promotes your business, you must think about it as the way to build long-lasting collaborative relationships.

That's why this book goes beyond the influencer marketing trend!

Going beyond the trend is why my business had such an amazing transformation, and I want you to experience the same.

My mission is to help you build unstoppable momentum and get your message out in a grander way, be recognized for your gifts, and create a truly magnificent business!

I structured the book based on the process I followed and continue to follow to build and nurture connections with influential people. I also delve into aspects of influencer marketing that my clients and prospects have identified as particularly important or challenging.

Strategies designed for service providers

The tactics you're going to learn are specifically geared for those who've built a business centered on their skills, experience, and expertise, such as coaches, consultants, practitioners, trainers, and other service providers.

Beyond the scope of this book is influencer marketing for business owners in manufacturing, retail, and e-commerce.

Because I wrote *Beyond Influencer Marketing* with such a targeted reader in mind, you'll feel that the strategies, examples, and stories within these pages really speak to you. You'll know exactly what to do to build long-lasting connections with influencers in your industry, and how to do it, too.

Clear signs this book can help you

If you can relate to any of the following challenges, *Beyond Influencer Marketing* **can help you.**

- You feel that it takes forever to prove yourself and create trust with your ideal audience.

- Potential clients say they can't afford your programs or that they need to ask someone else before they work with you—and you never hear back from them.

- You feel overwhelmed and frustrated after spending hours a day blogging, doing Facebook Live videos, and posting on social media to reach only a handful of people.

- You're tired of being the "best-kept secret" in your market.

- You don't want to depend solely on advertising to attract new clients.

And if you'd love to achieve the following, then Beyond Influencer Marketing is the book for you.

- Build authority exponentially.

- Connect with those ideal clients who appreciate your value, can afford your services, and are diligent enough to implement what you teach them.

- Generate revenue to support your ideal lifestyle while you make a positive impact.

- Feel empowered by the amazing possibilities unfolding before you.

- Leave a legacy for generations to come.

Not convinced yet?

If you've considered influencer marketing in the past but haven't followed through, or have shunned the idea of reaching out to influencers, you're not alone.

In fact, many entrepreneurs run for the hills when they hear the words "influencer marketing"! I often hear statements like:

- It's hard to gain the trust of influencers, especially since I'm just starting out with no proven results yet. Who am I to connect with influencers?

- It's too difficult to get past the gatekeepers and admins to connect with influencers.

- Influencers have big egos… I don't want to be chasing people.

- It takes a huge amount of time to get noticed by even one influencer. I already put in 12-hour days!

- It's hard to establish credibility without a book or something like a calling card.

- I've tried to reach out to influencers, but they ignore my emails.

- Why bother connecting with influencers when I'm probably going to be ignored or rejected?

Can you relate?

The truth... and my promise to you

Although common, the memes you just read are based on false beliefs. Kind of like the "five-second rule" to avoid getting sick or "knocking on wood" to have good luck.

I'll show you that connecting with key market influencers is well within your reach, and achievable without working 60-hour weeks.

In fact, my influencer marketing efforts take less than two hours a week!

Reading *Beyond Influencer Marketing* will help you achieve success with influencer marketing through adopting the correct mindset and applying my proven strategies.

When you read *Beyond Influencer Marketing*, you'll discover how to:

- Avoid common roadblocks to connect with influential people

- Assume a winning mindset that leads to measurable success

- Create a solid marketing foundation and become "influencer ready"

- Build and nurture long-lasting business relationships

- Tap into your network of connections to land your ideal clients

- Develop and implement a course correction when your influencer marketing hits a bump in the road.

You'll also find, sprinkled throughout the book, the personal stories of successful entrepreneurs who've grown their business through influencer marketing. Their stories will inspire and encourage you as you implement the proven tactics you're about to learn.

By the end of the book, I promise you that you'll have a clear vision of how to include influencer marketing as an integral part of your business growth efforts. You'll be thrilled to get to work and start building your network! So, are you ready to let go of your fear and misconceptions about influencer marketing?

Are you ready to seize this opportunity to grow your business?

If you answered yes, then what are you waiting for? Turn the page to begin your magnificent journey!

PART 1

GETTING READY TO CONNECT WITH INFLUENCERS

Chapter 1

What Influencers Are and How They Can Help You

....

Influencer marketing principle #1: Building a strong network of influencer connections can transform your business—and your life.

....

According to the *Cambridge Dictionary*, an influencer is a person or group that has the ability to influence the behavior or opinions of others.[1]

In the pre-Internet era, only bestselling authors, television and movie celebrities, top artists, business moguls, world-class athletes, and politicians were considered influencers.

But times have changed...

In our era, YouTube show hosts might have as much—if not more—influence on the behaviors and purchase decisions of their audience than movie stars.

Take entrepreneurial expert, author, and speaker Evan Carmichael, who created a solid business centered around his YouTube show for entrepreneurs. With more than a million subscribers, Evan's show has helped him land major consulting agreements, a book deal, and lucrative speaking engagements.

What if you wanted to reach entrepreneurs and Evan introduced you to his audience? What would that do for your business?

Consider Adriene Mishler and her Yoga with Adriene YouTube channel. With more than 2 million subscribers, Adriene's show serves as a platform to sell online yoga classes, a yoga clothing line, and tickets to her live events.

What if you were a health coach who wanted to connect with yoga enthusiasts, and Adriene introduced you to her audience? What would that do for your business?

Putting your business aside, what would connecting with people who've had such a high level of success do for your ability to believe that the same is possible for you?

Think of influencers as people who lead any engaged group that includes your target clients or customers. Their audience could be millions, thousands, or even hundreds ("niche influencers").

Leaders of local Meetups or coaches with 1,000 subscribers are influencers, as long as they're reaching your potential clients or customers. That's when the possibilities for you to benefit from influencer marketing exponentially expand.

Consider this…

For over 10 years, I ran an academic coaching and test prep company for high school and college students. I would help them with standardized testing, college applications, college essays, and resumes. I coached nearly 500 young people, some of whom made it to Ivy League schools such as Harvard and Yale.

Throughout a big chunk of that time, my average ad spending was only 5 percent of my revenue, and after a few years, I no longer needed to advertise at all.

How did I do that?

I created strong connections with guidance counselors in my town and surrounding areas. The counselors knew and trusted me, so they would send me potential clients who, because a counselor had referred them, didn't need much convincing to invest in my services.

At the time, I wasn't aware of the term "influencer marketing," but that's exactly what I had been doing. Those guidance counselors were the perfect kind of influencers for me because they had a captive audience of parents and students in the area where my business operated.

So, as you can see, influencers are all around you (online and offline).

Whether they have an audience of millions or hundreds, influencers can help you in three distinct ways:

- Instant authority-building

- Business growth

- Improving your perception of what's possible for you

Connections with influencers lead to instant authority-building

Think about your favorite podcast, blog, or Meetup. If the host, blogger, or group leader introduced you to someone, you'd pay attention. You would want to know more about the person, who, after all, knows a person you already admire, like, and trust.

Perception is everything.

In "Decoy," a video experiment done by Canon Australia, six photographers were invited to a man's portrait session.[2] Each of the photographers was told a different story about "Michael," their subject:

self-made millionaire, someone who has saved a life, ex-inmate, commercial fisherman, psychic, or recovering alcoholic.

All the stories were made up, and yet, the perceptions the photographers had of Michael completely changed the way they interacted with him and the outcome of their work. The video, with millions of views, shows the power of perception.

The video ends with the words, "A photograph is shaped more by the person behind the camera than by what is in front of it."

Your ideal audience will see you in a much more positive light when an influencer introduces you to them.

You stop being a stranger and become someone they want to listen to—someone they trust.

Connections with influencers result in business growth

If you've done the prep-work before you connect with influencers, you'll have a fresh stream of subscribers and clients.

Why? Consider this...

How do you usually make purchase decisions?

For most products, I look up the reviews on Amazon. I won't buy anything that has earned less than an average of 4 stars.

For services, I rely on TripAdvisor or Yelp. After I check the service's rating, I read the 3- and 2-star reviews to see what might be missing.

And for the most important service providers, such as doctors, lawyers, accountants, real estate agents, practitioners, and coaches, I ask for referrals.

I'm not alone...

In fact, according to a 2014 survey of small business owners conducted by Verizon and Small Business Trends, 85 percent of the respondents attracted customers through word-of-mouth referrals.[3]

Connecting with influencers has the power to generate a continuous stream of referrals for your business!

But if you're not prepared, your new connections might lead nowhere.

Think of the ABC television show "Shark Tank," where entrepreneurs pitch their business idea to billionaire investors such as Mark Cuban, Daymond John, Lori Greiner, Robert Herjavec, Kevin O'Leary, and Barbara Corcoran.

Many entrepreneurs miss out on a deal because they're indecisive, lack confidence, or don't know their numbers.

Some don't get a deal because they have a bad idea, such as "Wake 'N' Bacon," a wooden alarm clock that broils bacon at a preset time to wake you up. Fire hazard, anyone?

Other businesses miss out on a big portion of the "Shark-Tank Effect" by not being prepared to handle a huge spike in website traffic or a 1,000 percent increase in orders.

Some land a deal, but lack a long-term growth strategy, and end up going out of business.

You get the idea. Even with the help of the influencer "Sharks," success is not guaranteed.

However, business owners who prepare in advance and make the most of their visibility on "Shark Tank" can see exponential growth in their reach and their sales.

Although on a smaller scale, your business will also experience positive results when your target audience learns about you from an influencer. They'll feel much more compelled to work with you.

Connections with influencers change your perception of what's possible for you

When I started my radio show, I was inspired to spread my message of empowerment, but the little voice inside my head would often shatter my confidence. My fear of failure would rear its ugly head every time I checked the number of listens to my show and the visitors to my site.

My perception of what I could achieve started to change as I connected with my radio guests and bloggers. Many of them had faced more daunting challenges than mine, and yet, they had succeeded. They had started their businesses from nothing. Why couldn't I do the same?

Every day, as I built new connections, I felt more empowered. I opened my eyes to the possibilities ahead of me.

My increasing confidence spurred new ideas to grow my business and inspired me to implement those ideas.

Success is born from your own positive expectations. As Dr. Wayne Dyer said, "You'll see it when you believe it."

When you see yourself as capable of growing your business to the level you've always dreamed of, you'll have a real chance to make it happen. Surrounding yourself with successful, supportive people will help you create the mindset that results in positive action and tangible progress.

Connecting with influencers has been the best strategy I've applied to build authority and grow my business from scratch, and also what has inspired me to set high goals for myself.

My experience inspired me to write this book… because I know what connecting with influencers can do for you.

I hope that, by now, you're pumped up and ready to start!

Take action!

Step 1: Choose one word to describe the way you'll feel when you build a solid network of influential people.

Step 2: Write down your word on a post-it note and place it in your workstation where you will see it every day. You'll have a constant reminder of the reward that awaits you when you implement the strategies in this book.

Step 3: Download your bonus package ($197 value) to gain free instant access to ready-to-use templates and other valuable content to build your network of influencers. www.BeyondInfluencerMarketing.com/bonuses

Chapter 2

How to Overcome the Common Roadblocks That Prevent You from Connecting with Influencers

••

*Influencer marketing principle #2: You decide
if common roadblocks will stop you from
connecting with influential people.*

••••••••••••••••••••••••••••••••••

Y ou might be thinking that it would be nice to connect with influencers, and you might be aware of what influencer marketing can do for you and your business, but still, you haven't taken action yet.

You're not alone! It's very common to avoid influencer marketing or to give up soon after you start.

In my experience working with hundreds of entrepreneurs, I've pinpointed seven stumbling blocks that prevent entrepreneurs from connecting with influencers.

Let's explore them...

Block #1: You don't know where to start

Just as you may want to write a book but can't get past the title, you might have the best intentions to connect with influential people, but have no clue what to do first.

One of the first influential people I connected with was Lori Deschene, founder and owner of Tiny Buddha, one of the largest personal development sites in the world.

At the time, I wanted to promote my self-help book, so my attention was focused on anything related to personal development.

One day, as I was going through my Facebook feed, I spotted a Tiny Buddha article that a friend had shared.

I learned that Tiny Buddha was a site based on content from contributors who were eager to share their personal story. A bit more research showed me the incredible size of Tiny Buddha's readership, which at the time was a perfect match for my ideal audience.

I set a goal to publish one of my articles on Tiny Buddha, because I knew that if the site posted my articles, I would reach an audience of millions.

After reading their guest posting guidelines, I got to work. I wrote a personal story and lessons that seemed like a good fit for Tiny Buddha readers. I took the time to double-check that I was meeting every guideline before writing my pitch and hitting "send."

A reply soon popped up in my inbox. Lori said she'd love to publish my post!

That was the first of many posts, and the beginning of a friendship, too.

As "lucky" as it may seem, the impulse that drove me to learn more about Tiny Buddha wasn't random...

See, I once interviewed Anita Moorjani, a world-renowned author who writes about her near-death experience. Anita told me that her experience helped her realize that we exist in this vast space, like a huge warehouse, filled with all kinds of objects, information, people, etc.

Anita added that it's impossible for our brain to focus on everything that surrounds us at the same time. Instead, we're equipped with a proverbial "flashlight," which we point toward the topics that are top of mind. Sometimes we place all our attention on what's wrong with our life, so that's what we can see. We don't notice the solutions or opportunities that might be next to the obstacles. It's only when we decide to point the flashlight toward solutions and opportunities that we get truly inspired ideas.

I set myself up for success by placing all my attention on my ultimate goal: to reach people who were seeking inspiration and empowerment. That focus allowed me to see an opportunity to reach my ideal audience while browsing through my Facebook feed. I pointed my flashlight in the right direction, and that's how I learned about Tiny Buddha.

And that's what you can do, too.

Where do you want to point your flashlight? What do you want to achieve in your business and what kind of audience do you want to reach?

As you can see, your first step is as simple as keeping your eyes peeled for influencers in your topic of expertise, for people who already reach your ideal audience.

Block #2: You feel intimidated by it

It's amusing to see how the audience members of the "Ellen Show" react when they're selected to play a game or simply to meet Ellen DeGeneres, the host.

They scream, they jump up and down, they cry, they shake.

Their behaviors reflect their strong emotions, triggered by their perception of what Ellen represents.

If I sat on that stage and asked an audience member to meet me, they would probably tell me to wait until they finished going through their Instagram feed.

Ultimately, Ellen and you and I are just people. Yes, Ellen has amassed a fortune and reaches millions of people daily, but she and all other influencers have the same human needs and struggles as you and I. As someone once said, "We all poop." So true.

Connecting with influential people is only slightly different from connecting with anyone else. They tend to be approached often, sometimes by people without the best intentions, so they have built "walls" for protection.

Those walls could be tangible (gatekeepers) or intangible (reticence to accept requests from strangers).

You can slowly break down the walls by proving that you have good intentions. I'll show you how to do that.

But first, you have to let go of the feeling of intimidation you might be experiencing.

Remember, they're just people. You're just getting to know new people.

Block #3: You dread spending long hours in the process and failing anyway

One of the most common misconceptions about connecting with influential people is that it takes too long.

A life coach once said to me, "I know that it would help my business, but I already put in 12-hour days. How can I find the huge amount of time it takes to do influencer marketing? And what if the influencers ignore me and I waste my time?"

The same can be said about any marketing effort, including podcasting, blogging, creating video content, posting on social media, and orchestrating email marketing campaigns.

You *could* spend endless hours on those strategies.

And yes, you *could* fail even if you bust your butt.

But if you *focus* on what works, then not only will you save time and effort, but you'll get a positive return on your investment.

As Steve Jobs said, "That's been one of my mantras—focus and simplicity. Simple can be harder than complex: You have to work hard to get your thinking clean to make it simple. But it's worth it in the end because once you get there, you can move mountains."[4]

Building a solid network of connections will require commitment, time, and effort, but with the proven system and strategies you'll learn in this book, you'll be able to build your influencer network by investing *only a couple of hours a week.*

I typically spend less than two hours a week building and nurturing my network.

When I have upcoming interviews, speaking engagements, or guest appearances, I dedicate more than two hours to influencer marketing. However, because I'm only saying yes to forms of collaboration that can move my business forward, it's worth the time investment.

Block #4: You give up too quickly

Here are just a few examples of extraordinary people who didn't take no for an answer.

Stephen King had his first novel rejected by publishers 30 times. He continued pitching, until Doubleday said yes. Today, King has sold hundreds of millions of books, many of which have been made into successful films.

Jay-Z was rejected by several record labels and started to sell CDs out of his car, ultimately creating his own independent label. That independent label eventually led to a distribution deal that propelled the meteoric rise of his brand. Now, he tops the Forbes list of the most influential people in the world.

Entrepreneur Estée Lauder, in the early days of her business, was chasing a deal with Galeries Lafayette, Europe's largest department store. Even after landing a meeting with the store manager, she was rejected. But instead of giving up, Estée kept her "opportunity radar" on high alert. As she was making her way through the store, she noticed there was a crowd participating in a demonstration. So she "accidentally" spilled some of her Youth Dew on the floor. Everyone wanted to know what the fragrance was and how they could buy it, which left the manager with no choice but to welcome Estée Lauder's products into his store.

As you probably noticed, the common denominator in all these stories is perseverance.

If you continually support an influencer, they'll eventually take notice. If you give up too soon, you'll reinforce your own belief that influencer marketing is not for you or that it doesn't work.

I had been following and interacting with a top Canadian LinkedIn expert for over six months when I approached her to be a guest on my show. She said yes in an instant, and later told me that even though she had cut back on accepting interview requests, she said yes to me out of gratitude and appreciation.

To succeed, you need to be persistent while delivering as much value as possible. You also need to know when it's time to give up. We'll talk about that later.

Block #5: You pursue celebrities only

If you send your book to Oprah only, and place all your hopes on connecting with her as the way to get readers, it's highly likely that you'll be waiting a long, long time to reach your goal.

It's common to think of well-known celebrities when you hear the word influencer. However, "niche" influencers can be as powerful as celebrities when it comes to getting new clients.

Niche influencers—such as hosts of podcasts with small followings, bloggers, coaches, trainers, and leaders of Meetup groups—have very targeted and engaged audiences that you can reach in a much easier and faster way.

I encourage you to think of influencers not just in terms of the size of their audience, but in terms of the quality of their audience. If they reach exactly who you want to reach, then there's potential for collaboration.

Block #6: You pursue the wrong kind of influencer

Imagine a country music artist trying to reach the audience of rapper Nicki Minaj, or a business coach speaking about revenue models in a meeting of Mothers Against Drunk Driving.

I've exaggerated the mismatch to highlight the futility of initiating influencer efforts if you aren't clear on the audience you need to reach.

As much as I love to write about personal development, I had to say goodbye to posting articles on Tiny Buddha. Why? Because my business objectives had changed, as had my audience.

Instead of wanting to reach people who were going through a life challenge, I wanted to reach entrepreneurs and help them grow their business online. So I switched gears, and changed my influencer marketing strategy.

I'm still friends with Lori Deschene, but the time I spend on influencer outreach and collaboration is focused on those influencers who target my ideal audience. For example, I now write for the blog of Jeff Bullas (social media marketing,) Top Dog Social Media blog, Addicted2Success, and All Business Experts.

Selecting the right kind of influencer for your business is part of the foundation of your influencer marketing strategy, which we'll cover in more detail later.

Block #7: You've assumed the wrong mindset

Designing and applying an influencer marketing strategy with the wrong mindset will lead to poor results. Contrary to what most people might believe, the right mindset goes well beyond being positive, patient, and persistent. That's why I've dedicated the next section of this book to the topic.

It's tempting to skip through the mindset chapter and jump to the strategies for leveraging your connections to get more clients and make a bigger impact. I get it. You want to see the raving testimonials from your new clients—fast. You want to see the money in the bank!

But, as Abraham Lincoln said, "Give me six hours to chop down a tree and I will spend the first four sharpening the axe."[5]

Take the time required to adopt the right mindset and to build the foundation for a successful influencer marketing strategy, and you'll see the results you most want—and more!

Take action!

Step 1: Out of the seven common stumbling blocks, which one resonated with you the most?

Step 2: Write down one change in your thinking or behavior that will help you overcome that obstacle from now on.

Step 3: Commit to applying this change for the next 30 days so that it becomes a new habit.

Chapter 3

The Mindset Required to Connect with Influencers: Five Core Beliefs to Help You Succeed with Influencer Marketing

....

Influencer marketing principle #3: When you prepare to connect with influencers with the belief that you can succeed, you will succeed.

....

Mahatma Gandhi said:

"Your beliefs become your thoughts,

Your thoughts become your words,

Your words become your actions,

Your actions become your habits,

Your habits become your values,

Your values become your destiny."[6]

How's that relevant to your influencer outreach efforts? Well, your beliefs and thoughts about leveraging connections with influencers will become your results.

There are five core beliefs you need to adopt to succeed with influencer marketing.

Core Belief #1
You have value to offer

It's common to think that because you don't have tens of thousands of subscribers or a bestselling book, no influencer will want to connect with you. However, even if your business is in its early stages, you already possess value that you can offer to an influencer (or to anyone)!

That value is the combination of your knowledge, experience, and expertise, or as I often call it, *your magnificence*. And that doesn't mean that you need to be the top expert in a particular field to be ready to offer this value.

When I was growing up, my teenage cousin used to babysit me. My cousin was my hero. I wanted to be just like her. One day, we were playing with Barbie dolls, and she offered to teach me how to braid their hair.

I listened intently to each word, and watched every move as she skillfully braided the long brown hair of Ashley, my favorite Barbie. She gestured to another doll, "Now *you* do it."

To my surprise, I was able to braid the doll's hair as if I had been doing it all my life! I went on a braiding binge, unable to stop myself from braiding the hair of every doll in my cousin's home. I'll never forget that day.

Was my cousin the best hair braider in the world? No. Did she have a PhD in braiding or a bestselling book on the subject? No. She simply had a skill I didn't have.

She was one step ahead of me, and, in my eyes, that made her an expert.

Your unique set of experiences, insights, and education make you an expert. You must own this expertise with confidence, and realize that you have great value to offer.

Core Belief #2
It's possible for you to connect with influencers

As Dr. Wayne Dyer says in *You'll See It When You Believe It*, "The only limits we have are those that we encourage with our belief in those limits."[7] In other words, if you believe you'll fail when you reach out to influential people, you will fail.

But saying over and over "Yes, I can do it" won't do much to help you change your negative expectations.

Instead, you need to prove to yourself that it's possible for you to succeed with influencer marketing.

There are two ways to get that proof:

1. By seeking inspiration from those who were in your situation, or even in a much worse situation, and succeeded despite their challenges.

2. By taking small risks that involve a high probability of success, so you can see tangible proof that success is within reach.

Let's explore those two approaches in more detail:

Seeking inspiration

You can find inspiring success stories on podcasts, memoirs, and blogs, where you'll learn about other people who have been successful implementing influencer marketing. Some of those stories are sprinkled throughout this book. (I asked some of my closest connections to share their personal experience with you.)

Let's start by considering bestselling author and founder of Hay House Publishers, Louise Hay. Louise had an unstable, violent, and impoverished childhood, but that didn't stop her from finding a way to reach her ideal audience.

Her early "niche influencer" connections were within the Church of Religious Science, where she attended training and became one of their most popular speakers. That was the platform that inspired her to counsel individuals, write her books, and organize the gay men support groups that allowed her to differentiate herself and attract media attention.

Dr. Wayne Dyer made *Your Erroneous Zones* one of the bestselling books of all time by using the niche influencer marketing approach. He embarked on a self-financed national tour to share his message on any radio show that would welcome him. His efforts included giving interviews in the middle of the night, and spending countless nights sleeping in his car. But soon enough, those appearances opened the doors to appearances on the "Tonight Show with Johnny Carson," which cemented his authority in the personal development field.

More recently, top podcaster John Lee Dumas attributes his success in large part to his connection with his mentor, Jaime Tardy, who opened the door to new connections with influential people. Those influencers eventually appeared on his podcast for entrepreneurs, EOFire. With millions of downloads, EOFire has become one of the top podcasts for entrepreneurs in the world.

Now, it's your turn...

Pay close attention to those who have succeeded with influencer marketing, and notice how they're not much different from you or me. Inspiring success stories are abundant—all you need to do is find them.

Taking small risks

Achieving success when you take small risks prepares you to take on bigger projects that may have a higher risk of failure.

A great way to get tangible proof that you can be successful is to reach out to local or niche influencers. Since you're likely to succeed, you'll reinforce the belief that connecting with influencers with larger audiences is a possibility for you, too.

A few examples of niche influencers you can reach out to are:

- Business librarian in your town
- Leader of a local Meetup
- Leader of a local networking group
- President of the local chamber of commerce
- Coach or trainer you've already met at an event or online group

Simply take one step and become keenly aware of your progress and success. In time, you'll believe you're capable of achieving your most ambitious goals related to connecting with influential people.

Core Belief #3
Influencer outreach is like a sales process

If you're in business, you're likely to be in sales mode every day (consciously or subconsciously). You're not only selling your products and programs, but your ideas and your vision.

The good news is that you probably have experience with some of the sales steps below, which you can apply to your influencer marketing efforts.

1. Determine the needs and wants of your market
2. Have a clear offer

3. Pinpoint the best sales approach

4. Address objections

5. Craft the perfect close

6. Follow up

Let's explore each step in detail.

Determine the needs and wants of your market

In influencer marketing, your target audience (referred to as an "avatar") is the leader you intend to connect with. You'll need to start by:

- Researching their story

- Discovering the topics they're passionate about

- Determining what you have in common with them

When I pitched to the EOFire podcast, I had never met the host, John Lee Dumas.

However, as a fan of the show, I knew that John was passionate about the importance of having a clear avatar when one starts a business. That's why he created "Jimmy," the ideal listener that represents "Fire Nation" (his listeners). When John figured out exactly who he wanted to reach with his podcast, he was able to bring in the perfect guests to empower the Jimmys of the world to create and grow their business.

Because I had made the mistake of not selecting a clear avatar early in my business (I just wanted to help "everyone"), I knew I had a story to tell that would resonate with John's audience.

That's exactly what I said in my pitch.

With that first pitch, I landed an interview on EOFire. That's an accomplishment that takes years for many and proves impossible for others.

That's why you need to take the time to learn as much as you can about the influencer you want to reach. Find commonalities that might help you build rapport.

It's important to note, however, that you must be authentic in your approach. Telling someone that you're an avid camper when you've never spent a second in a tent won't work.

Have a clear offer

Before you can sell something, you've got to know what you're selling. More importantly, you need to know how to clearly express the benefits of what you're selling in a compelling way.

The same philosophy applies to pitching your expertise and value to an influencer. You need to be 100 percent clear on the value you offer. Not only that—you need to be clear about what aspect of your value proposition will be most appealing to the influencers and their audience.

For example, I became a regular guest on one of Connecticut's television variety shows by pitching ideas that would resonate with their ideal viewers, such as stay-at-home parents and retirees.

The show, with a predominantly female audience, was a great fit for the message of personal empowerment I aimed to share in the early years of my online business.

When I pitched an idea for a business-related event at my local library, I explained how my expertise in digital marketing would be welcomed by small business owners in the area, who often feel overwhelmed by the options available to market and expand their business online. I also explained that having me as a guest speaker would bring more people to the library. I got an instant yes.

Even though you might have a broad range of qualifications and expertise, it's important to emphasize only what's relevant to the particular influencer you're trying to connect with.

Just as it's best to customize a resume and cover letter when job hunting, it's also wise to tweak your initial communication and even your bio when reaching out to influencers.

How can you customize your message? With a clear value proposition. In Chapter 4, you'll learn how to establish a clear value proposition.

Pinpoint the best sales approach

In sales, you need to know how to position your offer so that it's irresistible to your potential client. Also, good salespeople tailor their sales approach to the needs of each client.

In the same fashion, when you want to connect with influencers, you need a clear, customized strategy.

Your strategy will vary depending on the influencer's situation, and will include:

- The best choice of medium to reach out to them

- The most compelling reason for them to connect with you

- Tangible value you can offer to them and their business

We'll go into the outreach process in much more detail in Part 2. For now, focus on the customized nature of this approach.

For example, I used LinkedIn to connect with personal branding expert and renowned TEDx speaker Dorie Clark.

Why LinkedIn? Because by going through her public posts on that social media platform, I figured out she was a very active LinkedIn user.

Dorie had recently released a book. So, in my personalized LinkedIn invitation, I mentioned what I loved the most about her new book.

Please note that I had actually read the book and expressed what I sincerely appreciated about it. I can't emphasize enough the importance of authenticity in the influencer outreach process!

A day later, she accepted my invitation.

Once we connected on LinkedIn, I nurtured the relationship by sharing her posts and books with my network.

A few weeks later, a mix of common sense and intuition told me it was the right time to take the next step, so I invited her to be a guest on my show. I explained how her personal branding message was a good fit for my audience, and she promptly said yes.

Common sense always plays an important role in the outreach process. Just as you'll know the right time to ask a new friend to go for a run with you, or a potential date to go out for dinner, you'll know when it feels right to take the next step with an influencer relationship.

I helped Dorie share her message with my audience (who loved her interview on my show). Dorie also shared the interview with her followers, which helped me build authority and attract visitors to my site.

The story had a happy ending because I took the time to send a customized message to Dorie. You, too, will have to find the most effective approach to connect with the right influencers.

Address objections

When I help my clients create their irresistible offers online, I always ask them to list the most common objections that their prospects are likely to have. Then, we work together to find a way to address and overcome those objections.

I apply the same philosophy in my own business. When I created Lead Generation Academy, a program designed to launch one's business online, I knew that a common objection would be: "What if I don't have a product yet?"

That's why I created a special bonus training called "Products that Sell," in which I show the participants how to craft those first offers and position them so that they're irresistible.

The same idea applies to your influencer outreach. If you're trying to pitch a new topic to a blogger, but have never guest-posted before, you'll know that their objection will involve uncertainty about your ability to write a compelling post.

To get past that objection, you could include the first few paragraphs of your article or even the whole article as part of your pitch. You could also prove your writing skills by submitting links to top-quality articles you have posted on your own site.

The key is to ask yourself, "Why would this person be reluctant to connect with me?" and then provide a solution before the objection arises.

Craft the perfect close

Closing a sale is possible when you make your offer at the right time.

Consider this: No one will raise their hand if you burst into a bar and ask the crowd, "Hey, anyone want to marry me?" The same applies to the relationships you create with influencers. No influencer will want to connect with you and introduce you to their audience if your attitude is "gimme-gimme-gimme."

You must first take the time to:

- Nurture the connection
- Prove your positive intentions
- Demonstrate your expertise
- Clearly phrase your value proposition

That's how you'll get a positive response when you ask them for something.

It was only after months of supporting Chris Brogan, a top influencer in online marketing, that I invited him to be a guest on my show. I saw him speak at a conference, and emailed him to let him know the positive impression his presentation made on me.

Our relationship evolved as I subscribed to his digital newsletter, and often replied to that newsletter with my best insights. Chris always took the time to respond.

Also, because that newsletter is my favorite out of the dozens I receive, I promoted it to my audience as often as I could.

I knew when it was the right time to invite Chris to appear on my show. He said yes, and I gave the interview as much exposure as possible so that his business would also benefit from his guest appearance.

Follow up

In sales, following up is a must, and it's equally important in influencer marketing. Persistence pays off!

Now, there's a big difference between being persistent and being a stalker.

- Consistently supporting the influencer on social media with shares and insightful comments = **persistence**
- Messaging the influencer on Facebook every day = **stalking**
- Emailing the blogger or podcaster a week after your pitch = **persistence**
- Pitching the same topic to the same people every week = **stalking**

- Providing continuous value to the influencer in the form of reviews, ideas, feedback = **persistence**
- Repeatedly emailing the influencer to say you're "checking in" = **stalking**

You get the idea…

Does the follow-up process ever end? Not really, because even if the influencer has agreed to support you, you'll still need to nurture the connection. Remember, you're in the relationship for the long term.

When do you give up if the influencer ignores your messages or requests? We'll explore this in more detail in Chapter 14, titled "What to Do When Influencer Marketing Goes Wrong." For now, keep in mind that your decision will depend on the person you're trying to reach and how important it is for you to create the connection.

Consider Walt Disney, who, at the suggestion of his daughter, decided to adapt PL Travers's novel *Mary Poppins* into a screenplay. There was a snag, though: The British novelist wasn't interested in selling her work to Hollywood.

Disney persisted, visiting the author in London for years until she eventually agreed to sell the rights to her novel.

Why did Disney succeed?

Because he had a burning desire to create the movie. He wanted to deliver on the promise he had made to his daughter. He had a mission, and did what it took to achieve what he desired.

As Steve Jobs said, "I'm convinced that about half of what separates the successful entrepreneurs from the non-successful ones is pure perseverance… Unless you have a lot of passion about this, you're not going to survive. You're going to give it up. So you've got to have an idea or a problem or a wrong that you want to right that you're passionate about; otherwise, you're not going to have the perseverance to stick it through."[8]

❧

As you can see, learning to view influencer outreach as a sales process will help you treat your potential new connections as you would your most important customers and clients, and you'll see results.

Core Belief #4
You're helping influential people succeed

You may wonder whether influencers would even consider connecting with you given that you might not have:

- A large list of subscribers

- Tens of thousands of followers on social media

- A popular podcast

- A bestselling book

- A seven-figure business

- A specific prize or accolade

- Anything you might consider necessary to gain the attention of an influencer

However, even though you might not have many obvious selling points, there's always a way for you to offer value to the influencer.

What matters most is to want to deliver value in the first place.

See, if you reach out to influencers with a what's-in-it-for-me mindset, it's very likely that they will see right through it and you will not even be able to start a relationship. If you have already connected with influencers, and all you care about is how they will help you, you will probably not develop the kind of long-term relationship needed to grow a thriving business.

Instead, you must approach influencers with the primary desire to help. For example, when I first wrote to Dr. Wayne Dyer expressing my appreciation, I did it because I felt truly grateful. I had no hidden agenda. My sincerity came through in my written word.

Bob Burg and John David Mann write in one of my favorite books, *The Go-Giver*, "Your influence is determined by how abundantly you place other people's interests first." So true! On my podcast, "Beyond Influencer Marketing," Bob Burg explained how the "Go-Giver" philosophy works, so I invite you to check out the interview.

Whenever I approach people of influence, I ask myself, "What's the best way to deliver value to them? What's going on in their lives right now that I can help them with?"

If you adopt a philosophy of giving, reciprocity is likely to kick in. However, it's important that you be detached, because some influencers will not reciprocate right away. That's okay. You're in this for the long-term.

Ready to deliver value to influencers?

Here are four approaches to consider:

1.   **Help them expand their reach.** No matter how large their audience or following is, influencers want to reach more people. If you can help them reach even one more person, you'll be delivering value.

2.   **Help them build their brand.** Influencers need a consistent flow of social proof to maintain their influencer status, and you can support them through reviews and testimonials.

3.   **Let them know they're making an impact.** Most influencers aren't "in it for the money" only. There are purely money-driven influencers, but why would you want to connect with them if your goal is to make a difference in the lives of those around you? Influencers worthy of

reaching out to usually have a mission to change lives and leave a legacy. So if you let them know they're fulfilling their highest goals, they'll appreciate it.

4. **Help them grow their business.** Even though the mission of the influencer might be to bring about positive change and make the world a better place, contributing to the influencer's bottom line is critical, and will be appreciated. After all, without revenue, it won't be possible for them to continue making an impact over the long term.

Here are some ideas to get your creative juices flowing:

Help them expand their reach

Retweet their posts (and add an insightful comment)

Many influencers check their Twitter notifications. If you're active on Twitter, choose to receive notifications when the influencers post, and retweet their most valuable content along with your own insights on the topic.

I've connected with other coaches who supported me via Twitter in such a consistent manner that I felt compelled to check out their websites and LinkedIn profiles. I eventually got to meet them to explore ways to collaborate.

Share their content on other social media platforms and with your network

No platform is too small. You can make an impact by sharing the influencer's content on your social media pages, social media groups, and even on your personal profile (as long as you make your post public).

All audiences count. What matters is that your audience, whether large or small, be engaged and trust you.

Be sure to tag the influencers when you share their content. Also, always add a comment that shows your expertise in the subject *and* benefits the community. "Nice post" or "Thank you" won't make an impact.

Write an article inspired by their work and post it on your site

That's how I connected with an influencer in the survival space, Creek Stewart. I tweeted an article I had written about his Weather Channel TV show "Fat Guys in the Woods," and he immediately took notice.

Creek was so impressed with the article that he shared it across his social networks. He eventually appeared as a guest on my radio show, and our friendship continues to grow.

If you write an article inspired by the influencer's work, select the most appropriate medium to let them know. If they don't notice when you tag them on social media, email them a link to the article. Share the article with your subscribers, too, if you have an email list.

Also, consider paying a few dollars to promote your article on Facebook. For a couple bucks, you'll get people engaging with the post, going to your site, and learning about the influencer. It's always about going the extra mile to deliver value.

Have them as guests on your podcast, blog, or virtual summit

Having your own platform, such as a podcast, blog, summit, YouTube channel, or online group, makes it easier to help an influencer expand their reach. However, don't fall into the trap of relying on the influencer to promote the interview or article. Instead, treat their participation in your community as the main benefit and their promotional support as a perk.

Go the extra mile to drive people to the influencer's interview or guest post. For example, you could write an article about their interview, and then pay to promote it on Facebook, LinkedIn, or Twitter.

Another fun idea is to share image quotes from the interview on social media, and encourage your followers to comment with their main takeaway from the conversation. Tag the influencer if someone adds an insightful comment.

If you visit my website, you'll see that I've written articles about my show guests. Some of those articles go beyond writing "show notes." I write my own insights and reflections on the influencer's words, which makes the article more valuable to the readers. Those readers will be much more inclined to check out the influencer's work, which is one of my main goals. It's always about delivering value first.

Personal Story: Leveraging Your Own Platform to Connect with Influencers by JV Crum III

"While I'd been a successful entrepreneur who went from a financially challenged childhood to reaching my first million by the age of twenty-five, I was not known in the public arena as an influencer.

I became an influencer by writing a bestselling book (#1 in 34 categories and #1 on all of Amazon) and by developing a network of podcasts and syndicated radio shows that have an audience exceeding 12 million listeners in 194 countries. My primary podcast, Conscious Millionaire, was named as one of the Top 13 Business Podcasts by Inc. Magazine.

All this success attracted numerous A-Listers, NY Times authors, producers, and other well-known influencers to become guests on my shows. I then leveraged these relationships by inviting many of them to follow-up conversations to discuss ways in which we could do business. This led to numerous affiliate relationships, being invited onto summits, their shows, and stages to speak or be a panel member.

What was the high-profit leverage opportunity that resulted from these relationships (over 800 and counting)? I gained access to their lists and was introduced as a trusted expert. It also resulted in introductions to their influencer relationships, who also became influencer partners and friends. Many of these new influencers also became guests on my show, invited me to affiliate with them, and asked me to their events. This has become an infinitely expanding web of influence connections.

For example, a couple of years ago, an influencer guest on one of my shows made a mutual introduction to Steve Olsher, who is a NY Times bestselling author. This led to Steve being a guest on my show. Over a year later, Steve reached out to me. He was planning an event, 'New Media Summit,' at which he would be featuring top podcaster influencers. Steve asked me to be one of his guests, who he called 'Icons.'

I had Steve on my show again to promote the event, and this also led to his company becoming a paying sponsor of several episodes as well.

Then at the event, where I was featured on several panels, I made connections with other top influencers as well as participants at the event. The result? I invited over sixty new

*guests to the show, many of whom were A-Lister influenc-
ers. I was also invited to be a guest on over ten top podcasts
and radio shows. And, I was invited into a private, seven-
person mastermind designed for top podcasters.*

*In the first month of being a member of this mastermind,
I leveraged my new relationships with other influencers to
increase Conscious Millionaire's profits. I utilized an idea
that was provided by another member to book a $50,000
underwriter for one of my podcasts. That booking included
having an influencer that I met at Steve's event to be my
regular guest on the podcast. I was also invited by another
mastermind member to be on his stage and became an
affiliate sponsor for another member's event.*

*My recommendation: Create a platform that will give
you immediate access to influencers. This can then result
in you beginning both business and personal relationships
with them, just as I did. You could create a blog, e-book,
or print book in which you publish interviews with influencers who are experts in your field. Most influencers love
promotion, especially high-quality, free promotion. Who
wouldn't? You could also create a podcast, as I've done, on
which you interview influencers. Then ask them to have an
additional conversation about ways you could do mutually
beneficial business.*

*Three years ago, I wasn't well known and had only a few
friends who were true influencers. Today, I've interviewed
over 800 unique guests, and have developed not only business but personal relationships with hundreds of them who
are influencers. You, my friend, can do the same!"*

JV Crum III is the host of Conscious Millionaire Podcast, named by Inc. Magazine as one of the Top 13 Business Shows to listen to in 2017. JV is the author of the #1 bestseller *Conscious Millionaire: Grow Your Business by Making a Difference.* He holds graduate degrees in law, business, and psychology, and has multiple certifications in NLP and coaching. Learn more about JV at www.ConsciousMillionaire.com.

Help them build their brand

Connect with them on LinkedIn and write a recommendation for them

Most influencers have a LinkedIn profile, and even if they're not active on the platform, they're likely to see the notification about the new recommendation, and they'll appreciate your gesture.

Base your recommendation on the influencer's main message. You'll need to visit their website and identify their core mission and vision. For example, if you're recommending a leadership expert for entrepreneurs, mention his or her impact on your leadership skills.

When you let them know you have written a recommendation for them, ask whether they would like to make an edit, and promptly make the changes if they ask for them. In most situations, they will simply express appreciation and not ask for revisions. Best of all, you'll have paved the path to a growing relationship.

Post a review of their book on Amazon

When I want to connect with an influencer who's recently written a book, my first step usually is to write a review on Amazon. Whether the book has five or 500 reviews, a positive review is always appreciated. If you want to make an extra effort, record a video review.

Email the influencer to let them know you have posted the review, or share a screenshot of the review on social media and tag them. Give them the opportunity to let their audience know about the impact their book is making—which is of huge value to them as they grow their readership.

If you feel the book is of interest to your audience, you could post a review of the book on your blog, and then share it with the influencer and your audience.

Anything you can do to stand out and deliver added value will help you initiate and nurture your connection with influencers.

Post a review of their podcast on iTunes

Podcasters crave iTunes reviews, so yours will certainly be appreciated. Email the influencer or tag them on social media to let them know about the review and ask what else you can do to support the show. If they ask for your help sharing the podcast, then follow through! You'll be stacking value on top of value, solidifying your relationship with that influencer.

A word about reviews: It's easy to write "great podcast" or "great book," but those kinds of reviews don't create an impact. Instead, write an honest review based on a specific benefit you were able to draw from their content. For example, if the influencer hosts a podcast about self-publishing, and you were inspired to write your first book because of it, then mention that when you write your review.

If you have purchased their courses or attended their events and got positive results, offer to create a video testimonial for them

Video testimonials are the highest form of social proof for a business, so it's highly likely that the influencer will eagerly say yes to your proposal.

Here's a four-part structure I recommend for a powerful testimonial.

1. **You.** State your name and business information relevant to the course or event.

2. **Your "before."** What challenges (related to the course or event) were you facing?

3. **Your aha moment.** What did you learn from the influencer that changed your mindset or behavior?

4. **Your "after."** What results did you get after implementing the influencer's strategy or lesson? How have those results changed your life or business?

Here's an example:

You. State your name and business information relevant to the course or event.

Hi, I'm Cloris Kylie. I'm an influencer marketing specialist who helps entrepreneurs build a solid network of influencer connections to build authority and grow their revenue.

Your "before." What challenges (related to the course or event) were you facing?

Before I took "ABC course," I wasn't sure how to assemble a virtual team that would allow me to delegate and focus on what I do best. I had hired VAs that either didn't do their job or did a terrible job. Creating a team was becoming more overwhelming than having no help!

Your aha moment. What did you learn from the influencer that changed your mindset or behavior?

That's when I joined "ABC course" by "XYZ influencer," and I understood that I was hiring the wrong kind of VA. To get better results, I had to be willing to invest in a technical VA, who wouldn't have a steep learning curve and who'd be responsible for more than one task.

Your "after." What results did you get after implementing the influencer's strategy or lesson? How have those results changed your life or business?

> *Now, I'm happy to say that I have a virtual team that allows me to scale my business and keep it running smoothly even when I can't be there. I'm more than happy to recommend "XYZ" and her "ABC Course."*

Creating such a testimonial is one of the most powerful things you can do to initiate and nurture a relationship with an influencer.

Let them know they're making an impact

Most influencers have gotten where they are because of their deep passion to make an impact on the lives of those around them. If you show them that their efforts are paying off, they'll remember you. That's a perfect way to initiate a relationship with them. Below are a few ideas to spark your creativity.

Comment on the content they create

This includes:

- LinkedIn posts
- Facebook updates
- Facebook group posts
- Videos
- Blog articles
- Podcast show notes

When the influencer publishes new content, be one of the first to comment. You could mention your #1 takeaway from the content, share a previous related experience, and—if possible—add a valuable statement that shows your expertise on the subject.

I'm a fan of Kate's Take, the audio blog by Kate Erickson of EOFire. When I finish listening to a new episode of the show, I usually take a couple of minutes to go to the show notes and write my insights on the subject. That way, I let Kate know she's making a positive impact, and I also offer my ideas for future shows, which she appreciates. On one occasion, she even created an episode based on my suggestion. In addition, my comment inspires others to write their own comments, so we're all gaining value from sharing our feedback and personal takes on the subject.

Subscribe to their list and reply to their emails (if appropriate)

Influencers will sometimes ask their email readers to reply. Often, they personally read the replies, and they will appreciate your feedback. Also, the act of replying will help their email deliverability, keeping their messages from being diverted into spam folders. This tends to be a major issue for those who have huge mailing lists, such as top influencers.

Also, if the influencers share an exclusive newsletter with their audience, and the content strongly resonates with you, reply with your feedback. If they personally check their business email account (which happens more often than you think), they'll appreciate your gesture.

Replying to Chris Brogan's weekly newsletter allowed me to nurture my relationship with Chris, a top influencer. I found so much value and inspiration in the newsletter that it felt natural to reply. That's what you want. You never want to force yourself to write a reply, or to feign appreciation for the content of the email or newsletter. In that case, it's best to find another way to let the influencers know they're making an impact.

Help them grow their business

Would you be appreciative and want to learn more about someone who's an advocate of your message and does what it takes to help you grow your business? "Heck yeah!" you might be thinking. Influencers will feel the same way. That's why this is such an effective way to initiate and nurture your influencer connections. Here are some ideas to get you started.

Send them ideas that will benefit them and their business

This is a commonly overlooked way of delivering value, yet it's one of the most powerful!

Millionaire entrepreneur and author James Altucher calls himself an "idea machine." He not only creates a flow of daily ideas for his own business, but also comes up with ideas to help other people's businesses. He says that when he submitted his ideas to Amazon, the company flew him to Amazon headquarters to thank him and to hear more.

As Altucher says, "Give ideas for free, and then when you meet, give more ideas. And if someone wants to pay you and your gut feels this is a good fit, then give even more ideas."[9]

Remember, however, that influencers are often pressed for time, so be concise when you share your ideas with the influencer and offer to provide more details if they're interested.

What matters most when you approach the influencer is that you clearly express the idea and how it will help their business. Also, your ideas must be aligned with the core mission of the influencer, and that's where your knowledge of their business comes into play.

What's the best way to share your ideas? Email might work, but it is often routed to "gatekeepers" (for those influencers with large businesses) or simply lost in the shuffle. If you want to stand out, mail them a printed document or a USB drive with your ideas.

Another way to stand out is to send a video card. I've used a service called Spreengs, which allows you to create and mail a customized greeting card with your video.

I bet you can come up with your own way to deliver your ideas. Be creative, but never let a lack of creativity keep you from taking action. Once you take the first step, the next one will usually manifest itself.

Review their websites and notify them if there are broken links

Wouldn't you appreciate it if someone let you know your site wasn't working right? So will the influencers!

From time to time, I get an email from a reader about a website link that isn't working. Also, once I received an alert about a typo on one of my pages. Oops! What's the first thing I did? After I thanked them, I checked to see if they had a link to their website on their email signature so I could learn more about them.

If you use this strategy to connect with an influencer, your next step should be to continue nurturing the connection by following up with another way to deliver value. For example, if you've alerted influencers about a problem on their site, you could then post a review of their book (within a week of the initial communication) and email them to let them know. Next, you could write a comment on their blog, and so forth.

Buy their courses or group programs

Needless to say, one of the reasons influencers are as successful as they are is that they take care of their clients and customers.

If the influencer offers a course or program, becoming one of the participants will allow you to stand out and deepen your knowledge of their business and expertise.

I've connected with top influencers online by signing up for their training programs. By doing so, I gained knowledge from experts in my industry and created new connections.

It's easier than ever to apply this strategy now that many online programs include membership in a Facebook group. Once you've joined the group, become an active participant and contributor. Offer your best insights and seek answers to any questions you may have.

By becoming an active participant, not only will you nurture your connection with the creator of the course, but also with other participants, who might become future clients or business partners.

Attend their live events and introduce yourself

As powerful as online networking is, there's nothing like meeting someone in person to create and deepen a connection.

If a connection with an influencer is of utmost importance to you and your business, you should attend one of their live events.

Keep in mind that it might not be possible for you to meet them in person, unless it's during a book signing. However, you can use what you learned during the event to create a review that they'll be more likely to notice. By having participated in their event, you'll have a common experience with them that you can reference when you reach out to them on social media or via email.

If you attend an event led by niche influencers, it will be easier to talk to them during one of the breaks or socials that usually follow the day's sessions. When you introduce yourself, mention what you appreciate the most about them and the difference they have made in your life and business.

If you have a picture taken with them, tag them when you share the picture on social media.

Be mindful that the person is under pressure to deliver a high-quality conference, and he or she is likely to be approached by many people. That means it's best to not overextend your time with the influencer. Make it short and substantive.

As you can see, there's so much value you can bring to influencers that they'll be grateful they connected with you! Make sure you're aware of that value, and take focused action to deliver it.

Core Belief #5
You're building long-term connections

Imagine if you were an avid hiker, and had to make a new friend every time you wanted a hiking buddy for your Sunday hike. Exhausting just to think about it, right? That's why we tend to think of friends as people we get to know better and who hopefully will be in our life over the long term.

The same thinking applies to influencer connections.

To get a long-lasting benefit out of your influencer outreach efforts, you must support your connections regularly and create long-term relationships with them.

Try to view your relationships with influencers as evolving through distinct phases. I will summarize them into three main stages:

- Infancy

- Growth

- Maturity

Let's explore each of those phases and what you can expect in each of them.

Infancy

In the infancy stage of the relationship, the influencer becomes aware of you, and you experience the "mere-exposure effect," also called "familiarity principle." This psychological phenomenon involves the human tendency to develop a preference for things (or people) they see more often.

We all experience the effects of the familiarity principle daily. Let's say you go for a morning jog, and you see another jogger every day on the trail. You wave to each other and go on with your day. All else being equal, if you see that jogger you "know" and then a new person you have never seen before, you're much more likely to trust the jogger you see every day, even though you really don't know anything about him. He could be a serial killer, but you're more positive about him because he's more familiar.

That's why you'll need to make an extra effort to be present often in the influencer's awareness so that the relationship can get a solid start.

The process isn't only about creating familiarity, but about delivering value with integrity. Every interaction with the influencer should be like a deposit into their goodwill account.

That goodwill account will lead to the next phase of your relationship: growth.

Growth

During the growth phase, the influencer will create a positive expectation of your relationship with them. They'll trust in your support, and you'll become an ally in their eyes.

That's when influencers are most likely to want to learn more about you. For example, they'll be inclined to visit your website, meet you virtually or in person, or ask you for more information.

In this stage, influencers might agree to appear as guests on your own platform (podcast, YouTube show, Facebook group, etc.) and be open to listening to your ideas for collaboration.

Just as you need to water a plant regularly, you must continue to support the influencer on a regular basis so that, in time, you won't need to prove yourself anymore. Your actions should be driven by the desire to give without expecting anything in return.

Once the influencer trusts you completely, your relationship will move to the maturity phase.

Maturity

In this phase, it's likely that your connection will be compelled to help you without being asked, and won't hesitate to say yes if you ask for help.

It's in this phase when joint venture partnerships are formed, and also when you and the influencer become advocates of each other.

That's when you'll experience the maximum power that your connections have in the growth of your reach, the size of your list, and your revenue.

∽

Assuming a giving-first mindset with the ultimate goal of building a long-term relationship will help you avoid a common pitfall: rushing the relationship to such an extent that it turns off the other person.

Whenever you're tempted to rush, keep in mind that all the time and effort you have already put into the relationship could go to waste. Also, pay attention to how you feel before you take the "next step" with an influencer. If you feel uneasy or hesitant, it might be too soon. Wait and remind yourself that patience pays off.

Personal Story: Building a Network of Influencers One Tweet at a Time by Claire-Diaz Ortiz

"As an early employee at Twitter, I was part of a fast-growing startup with one big idea. That idea? Bringing onboard key 'influencers' in different regions and demographics and niches who would help to make Twitter a household name.

The theory, in short, was that a rising tide would rise all boats.

I said this time and again when I explained the work I was doing—flying and talking and courting and tweeting. Always the tweeting. I worked with politicians and celebrities and the Pope. Every time, I came to work with this one idea.

The idea—that all the boats will rise if we raise the tide—was one that encompassed everything good about what we were doing, and everything good about what influencer marketing could be.

It wasn't a strategy concocted in a boardroom or a transactional game where you get an influencer to do something for you and then you ran the other way, yelling 'Gotcha!' all the way.

Instead, it was an exchange set apart by a give-and-take that made all sides feel valued.

From my side, it was easy to buy in to the idea that we, as employees, needed to promote the product to key influencers. But once they are on, how do you make them stay? How do you keep them engaged, keep them tweeting, and keep them coming back for me? Interestingly, I soon found that it was my very connections with other influencers that made individuals and organizations stay on the platform.

Ultimately, I was doing influencer marketing before I knew influencer marketing was a thing, and it turned out so were many of the individuals I was working with. We were doing it because it worked, because when one boat rose, the others followed suit. Again and again, tweet after tweet."

Claire Diaz-Ortiz (@claire) is an author, speaker, and Silicon Valley innovator who was an early employee at Twitter. Named one of the 100 Most Creative People in Business by Fast Company, she holds an MBA and other degrees from Stanford and Oxford and has been featured widely in print and broadcast media. She writes a popular business blog at ClaireDiazOrtiz.com and is the award-winning author of eight books published in more than a dozen countries.

Take action!

Step 1: Write down the five core beliefs to succeed with influencer marketing. The act of writing them down will help them take root in your belief system.

Step 2: Based on the ideas you learned in this chapter, write down three actions you could take today to help influential people succeed.

Step 3: Refer to the list from step 2 and affirm with joy and conviction, "I'm ready to start long-lasting relationships with influencers to grow my business."

Chapter 4

The Three Components of a Solid Influencer Marketing Foundation for Long-Term Success

Influencer marketing principle #4: You'll get the most out of your influencer outreach when you build a solid foundation.

There's a story that has been in the local Connecticut news for years now: crumbling concrete foundations. The materials used to build the foundations are the largest contributors to the problem. The fixes tend to be so expensive that the cost of the repairs nearly matches what the owners paid for their home.

Imagine you buy a home and spend a fortune on flooring, siding, roofing, and tiling, thinking that you're investing in the future. And then you find out your entire home might collapse.

Not a pretty picture.

Now, imagine you spend precious time and effort trying to connect with the right influencers, but months or years later, you realize you've had the wrong approach all along. Or what if you manage to connect with an amazing group of influencers, but then you don't know how to tap into your new connections to make a bigger impact and grow your business?

As empowering as it is to connect with influencers, you also need to get tangible results in the form of subscribers, impact, and revenue!

As important as it is to adopt the right mindset before you start your influencer outreach, building a solid marketing foundation is a must if you want to succeed with influencer marketing. That's why, when I work with my clients, we first focus on strengthening their marketing foundation.

Showing you exactly how to build that foundation is outside the scope of this book, but I'll explain how each element of the foundation fits within your influencer marketing strategy.

The main components of your influencer marketing foundation are:

- Clear avatar
- A list-building system that leads to your product or program
- Unique value proposition

Clear avatar

Although connecting with Garth Brooks might be interesting and exciting, that connection will probably not help you grow your money-coaching business. Yes, Garth probably has plenty of followers who could use your advice for financial success, but they don't see Garth as someone who could introduce them to a money-management advisor.

In contrast, if you're starting a career as a country music singer, then Garth would be an ideal connection for you.

That's just an extreme example to show you how important it is to define your ideal avatar and that of the influencer to see if there's a match.

In most cases, the answer isn't that simple. For example, if you're a business coach who serves software startups, attempting to connect with influencers whose audience is e-commerce entrepreneurs would not be the best idea. However, connecting with the host of a podcast for SaaS entrepreneurs would be perfect for you.

Find the following qualifiers about your ideal avatar before you select your influencer connections. If most of your answers match the description of their audience, then you should reach out to them.

Keep in mind that some of the qualifiers might not be relevant for your market. Focus on what will make a difference in defining who is and isn't an ideal client for you.

1. Gender

2. Age group

3. Annual income

4. Level of education

5. Occupation

6. Preferred social media platform

7. Favorite blog

8. Top podcast, TV show, or YouTube channel

9. Favorite book and magazine

10. What groups or associations do they belong to?

11. What certifications or degrees do they have?

12. What's their greatest single challenge (related to your service or product)?

13. What's their primary goal (related to your service or product)?

Use the data to create a complete avatar profile. Then, thoroughly research the influencer's audience and compare it to yours. That's how you'll be able to tell if that person is a good match or not.

A list-building system that leads directly to your product or program

To get tangible results out of your influencer outreach efforts, you need to have an effective list-building system Why? Because, just like advertising, influencer marketing will bring people (aka traffic) to your site. If you have nothing to offer your website visitors in exchange for their email address, they'll leave to probably never come back.

Your list-building system should include:

- **A free offer (lead magnet)**
- **A compelling landing page where people can access your free offer**
- **An email sequence to welcome new subscribers**

Let's briefly cover each element of the system.

A free offer (lead magnet)

With opt-in rates that tend to be less than 1 percent, "Subscribe for Updates" forms are not an effective way to grow your list. Business owners must provide a specific valuable offer to their new subscribers.

If you land an appearance on a podcast or a guest-posting opportunity, you'll get the best results if you're ready to provide a downloadable gift (lead magnet) related to the topic covered.

We're not talking about any kind of lead magnet, but one that is created with the customer journey in mind. If you're a weight-loss coach, a free recipe book for lean cooking—when your goal is to sign up people for your new exercise program—won't be effective.

Each of your paid offers should have a corresponding lead magnet, unless all your products solve the same problem. In that case, it might be enough to offer only one gift.

For example, if you offer a digital training course to quit smoking, but also offer private coaching to achieve the same result, then your free offer could be the same.

Examples of lead magnets include:

- Cheat sheet
- Blueprint
- Challenge
- eBook
- Self-assessment quiz
- Video
- Mini-class (via email or video)
- Webinar or teleseminar
- Coupon for a special discount

Usually, the "highest converting" free offers (meaning those for which people tend to opt-in the most) are those that provide immediate satisfaction. That's why a webinar might not bring in as many subscribers as a cheat sheet.

In most cases, your conversion rate (number of people who sign up for your list) will be indirectly proportional to the time it will take people to get an answer to their main question or issue.

- Less time to get an answer and consume the content = higher subscriber rate

- More time to get an answer and consume the content = lower subscriber rate

Be clear about how your free offer will be of value to the influencers' audience, and be ready to explain its value when you share your message with that audience.

Your free offer may also be part of your referral kit, which you can provide to your connections so they can introduce you to potential clients.

A compelling landing page where people can access your free offer

The landing page is the webpage where potential subscribers enter their information to access the gift. A landing page that isn't compelling will thwart your list-building efforts.

To help you design compelling lead magnets and landing pages, I've included an easy-to use lead magnet guide and landing page template in the book's bonus package. Just go to **www. BeyondInfluencerMarketing.com/bonuses** and sign up to access all the bonuses, including this guide.

You could create a landing page exclusively for the influencer's audience. For example, I created a landing page only for listeners of my interview on EOFire. That customized page, with a headline that read "Special Offer for Fire Nation," made visitors feel they were accessing something specifically designed for them, which greatly helped the sign-up rate.

Make sure you have a way to track the results of each guest appearance and other forms of collaboration with influencers.

If you have a Wordpress site, you could use a plugin to create customized URLs per influencer, which will allow you to track the number of clicks to your landing page accurately. For example, if I were to appear on the Passive Income Podcast, I would create a URL such as cloriskylie.com/passiveincome.

You could also track your results with UTM parameters, affiliate links, or other software tools. The tracking process might seem daunting to you, but don't let the technology intimidate you. Either overcome the learning curve or hire an expert to help you.

Email sequence to welcome new subscribers

People are signing up for your free offer. Your list is growing. Now what?

If you wait weeks to follow up with your new subscribers, they'll probably forget they signed up for your list. Not only will this make them likely to unsubscribe, but they may select "spam" as a reason for their decision to leave your list, which will damage the deliverability of your emails.

When you receive several subscriber complaints, your messages are more likely to be sent to the spam folder. Even worse, your email management software account could be shut down.

That's why, before you're introduced to the influencer's audience, you must have written and programmed the welcome email series for new subscribers.

I suggest you have a minimum of three emails in the series: a welcome email and two follow-up messages.

Your welcome email should include:

1. A little about who you are

2. What to expect from you (content, email frequency)

3. A link to download the gift you're offering

You might send your first follow-up email two or three days later. Include a new resource related to the original gift.

Your second follow-up email (sent two or three more days later) might include a different resource that reinforces your authority.

Depending on your goal, you might want to add more emails in this automated series. You could send your clients' success stories. Your goal isn't to brag, but to show your subscribers what they could achieve if they became your clients and customers.

After your initial email series, you'll continue to communicate with your new subscribers through regular email campaigns.

Just as you created and nurtured your relationship with the influencers, now you're building a relationship with their audience. The same principle applies: Deliver as much value as possible.

If you decide to create a customized landing page for a specific audience, you might also want to create a customized welcome email series for your new subscribers.

However, keep in mind that customization will always add complexity to your business. Before you promise a customized offer, page, and email sequences to an influencer, be sure that the audience is large and targeted enough so that you'll get enough subscribers in exchange for your efforts.

A good benchmark for me is a minimum of 100 potential subscribers to create a customized page, and 300 potential subscribers to create a customized email sequence. Your benchmark might be different depending on your niche audience and industry.

Unique value proposition

The last element of your influencer marketing foundation is your unique value proposition.

According to Unbounce.com, "Also known as a unique selling proposition (USP), your Unique Value Proposition is a clear statement that describes the benefit of your offer, how you solve your customer's needs and what distinguishes you from the competition."[10]

There are two main components of your unique value proposition:

1. Your offer

2. The uniqueness of your offer

Let's explore each of those elements.

Your offer

Your offer is the value you can potentially bring to the influencer and to their audience.

To expand on what you learned in the "You Have Value to Offer" section in Chapter 3, here's a list of examples to help you come up with creative ways to bring value to your influencer connections.

Your social media platform

Just like you, influencers are interested in expanding their reach, so you can provide great value if you have an engaged community of social media followers who would appreciate the influencer's core message or offers.

Ways to share the influencer's message with your online community include:

- Adding a personal message when sharing posts and videos

created by the influencer, explaining how the content has helped you and/or can be of value to your audience

- Hosting a Facebook Live interview with the influencer on your Facebook page or Facebook group, where you tell the viewers why they would benefit from connecting with the influencer and where to find more information about him or her

- Creating a Facebook Live video with your opinion about the influencer's recent book or program emphasizing the benefits for your audience

I have applied all of these strategies with positive results. I once created a short series of Facebook Live videos on my Facebook business page I called "Mag Snack," where I shared "a snack, an inspiring story to help entrepreneurs build a magnificent business, and a resource to do just that."

I invited influencers as guests for informal 10-minute interviews, where the resource would be a free download offered by my guest. I delivered value to my guests and to my Facebook audience, who learned from the insights shared on the mini show. I also embedded the videos on a single page and shared them with my subscribers.

Are the ideas flowing yet? What could you do on social media platforms to offer value to an influencer?

You must avoid anything that could be seen as "spammy," such as sharing a link without any of your personal opinions about it on all social media sites or on multiple groups.

Whatever you decide to do on social media, be sure it's a win-win for both the creators and the consumers of the content.

Your list of subscribers

One of the most powerful ways to support an influencer is to introduce them to your subscribers. In contrast to social media, you have control over who on your list sees your messages and when they see them.

If you've segmented your list, you'll be able to select the group who might be most interested in what the influencer has to offer, maximizing the value for the influencer and for the recipients.

Don't be discouraged if your list is small. Usually, smaller lists have much higher open and click-through rates than large lists, so you can get even better results with a promotion if you've built a good relationship with your small list of subscribers.

One of my connections became a top training program's most successful joint venture partner even though she had a relatively small list of subscribers (fewer than 2,000 people). She had a close connection with her list, so when she sent a personalized message to selected subscribers about the program, the response was extraordinary. Her success supporting that program opened the door to many new influential connections. Now she has tens of thousands of subscribers and a booming business.

Your podcast, YouTube show, virtual summit, or blog

Having a content platform of your own is one of the simplest ways to offer value to an influencer. Here are some examples to inspire you.

Podcasts and YouTube Shows

I met a large chunk of my influencer connections through "Magnificent Time," my first online radio show. In fact, I landed my first television appearance because, in my pitch, I mentioned that I had an online radio show with world-renowned guests.

As I grew my business, I made a point to invite my new influencer connections to appear on my show. That proved to be a powerful way to nurture those relationships.

When I transitioned to broadcasting on my "Beyond Influencer Marketing Podcast," I brought in old and new connections to share their influencer marketing insights.

Many of my guests are podcasters or YouTubers themselves, and when I ask them, "What's your most effective way to connect with influencers?" they usually answer, "My show!"

Virtual Summits

A podcast can make it easier for you to organize virtual summits or live conferences. For example, Coach Marie Grace Berg leveraged her podcast to find guests for her series of virtual summits. Those events allowed her to rapidly build her list by the thousands each time she hosted them, and to boost her revenue well into six figures in less than a year.

Blogs

Your blog can also become an effective tool to deliver value to your connections. You could post one of their articles, or instead you could write an article inspired by their story or their insights.

In the third year of my first radio show, I started to post short blog articles based on my guests. I enhanced the posts by adding a link to the audio and video recording of the corresponding interview. That way, I would spread my guests' message in three different ways (text, audio, and video.)

My blog allowed me to connect with survival expert and TV personality Creek Stewart. As a fan of his survival show on the Weather Channel, "Fat Guys in the Woods," I realized that surviving in the wilderness required skills akin to those needed to survive and thrive in business.

I was moved to write about how the basic principles of survival could be applied to entrepreneurship. My website saw a huge spike in visitors when Creek shared the article on all his social media platforms.

Months later, he appeared as a guest on my first radio show, and our friendship continues to grow. Now, he's contributing his own influencer marketing story to this book.

Personal Story: Associating with Influencers to Create a Movement and Skyrocket Your Career as an Expert by Creek Stewart

"I started my survival training business in college and operated it for about 12 years without any web presence at all. As can be imagined, it was incredibly challenging to acquire exposure and new customers by word of mouth, posting flyers in local outdoor retailers, and sending press releases to local newspapers.

I knew that to really grow my business I needed more exposure and the natural place for this was on the Internet. So, I started a blog and wrote articles about what I knew— wilderness survival skills.

Much to my disappointment, I (along with a few of my family members) were the only ones reading my content. While I very much appreciated the comments that my mom and brother left on my articles, I knew this was headed nowhere fast.

I decided to reach out to blogs with a broader influence than mine who had a viewership that might also have an interest in survival skills. I was naïve at the time, which, looking back, really worked in my favor. I didn't ask them for anything—no links, no referrals, nothing. I didn't even know to ask that. I just simply emailed and asked them if they would be interested in posting an exclusive article that I would write about a survival skill that their readers may be interested in learning. My goal was to just have more people read my articles and then hopefully Google me to find out more information if they were interested.

After sending more emails than I could count, I actually got a reply! It was from a huge men's interest blog that had a following at least a thousand times that of my own. The owner of that blog, who I am still indebted to this day, asked if I would write an article about how to build a bug out bag disaster survival kit. I quickly agreed, dedicated my life to that task, and submitted the article about a week later. He asked me to include a simple byline about myself, which I was happy to do. The byline included a link to my blog at www.willowhavenoutdoor.com.

That single article led to many thousands of new visitors to my website, tons of new students in my survival classes, additional requests to write articles from other blogs, and a book deal for my first book titled Build the Perfect Bug Out Bag, which is still to this day an Amazon bestselling title.

The moral of the story is that if you want to grow your reach, try to associate yourself and your brand with other brands that have a similar market with a broader reach than your own. Make an offer to provide them with content, with abso-lutely no expectation of anything in return. Then, deliver them incredible content. The rest will take care of itself.

Remember, it's not IF but WHEN.

CR///EK Stewart, a survival expert, has been featured in local and national media outlets such as the "Today Show," "Inside Edition," "Fox & Friends," Men's Fitness Magazine, Backpacker Magazine, Outdoor Life Magazine, and The Weather Channel. He's a regular contributor to ArtofManliness.com, and his writings have been featured on websites with millions of readers, including Huffington Post, MSN News, Lifehacker, and The Daily Beast. Creek is also the host of the hit series on The Weather Channel "Fat Guys in the Woods" and "SOS: How to Survive." Some of his bestselling books are *Build the Perfect Bug Out Bag, Build the Perfect Bug Out Vehicle,* and *Survival Hacks.* Creek owns and is the lead instructor at Willow Haven Outdoor Survival School in Central Indiana, where he manages APOCABOX, his bi-monthly subscription survival box. www.CreekStewart.com.

Your network

As you build your audience and connections, the network itself will play a strong role in your value proposition. I nurture my relationships with many of my influencer connections simply by introducing them to the right people.

You could introduce your connections to:

- Podcasters who could have them as guests on their show

- Bloggers who could feature their articles

- Guests for their podcast or YouTube show

- Potential clients

- Potential JV (joint venture) partners

Every time I meet someone new, I ask myself, "Who do I know that they would want to meet?" And then, after I run the idea by them, I make the introduction.

Warning: Introductions can become a time-consuming task. To save time, create a simple Word document with a short bio for all of your top influencer connections. When it's time to make an introduction, simply copy and paste the bio into the intro email.

Remember that intros also require time and effort from the people who are being introduced to each other, so before you make the introduction, always ask them if they'd be interested in it.

I've received out-of-the-blue introduction emails at the busiest times in my business. As a result, I couldn't take the time to build and nurture the new relationship. To be safe, always ask.

The formula I use for my intro emails is included in **the book's bonus package**. Just go to **www.BeyondInfluencerMarketing. com/bonuses** and sign up to access all the bonuses, including the "Intro Email Formula."

Finally, be mindful of the reason for the introduction and express it clearly (and authentically).

I was once introduced to a woman who was presented to me as a potential client. To my surprise, she said she had never expressed interest in connecting with a marketing coach.

The misunderstanding placed both of us in an awkward situation. Introducing people on false or misleading premises doesn't help anyone.

Your products and services

Yes, your paid offers can be of value to an influencer!

Influencers most likely have become influencers because they do one thing very well. But that doesn't mean they do *everything* well.

Their audience has unmet needs that the influencers can't or don't intend to satisfy.

That's where you come in.

If you have an offer that complements the influencer's offers, you have a solid opportunity for collaboration.

However, you shouldn't start a relationship with an influencer by talking about your products, but about the expertise you offer in the subject. Your goal at the beginning of the relationship is to prove yourself as an expert in your field.

As your relationship matures, you'll be able to explore JV partnerships with the influencer. If you create such a partnership, the influencer will introduce your free offers to their audience. Those free offers will, in turn, lead to your paid products and programs. The influencer will benefit from the added value delivered to their audience, and from the commission earned from the sales generated by their campaign.

The key is to make your paid programs and services so focused on solving a specific problem that there's minimum overlap between what you offer and what your potential partner offers.

I've connected with coaches and trainers who serve a similar audience to mine and who could have become joint venture partners. However, their offers were so broad (e.g. a "complete online marketing guide") that it wasn't possible for us to collaborate.

The more you focus, the more you win!

Your ideas

Your ideas are like currency you can use to "buy" an influencer's attention.

Even if you don't initiate the connection by sharing your ideas, it will be helpful to outline potential ideas that might benefit the influencer in the future.

When I visit people's websites or social media pages, I put on my "marketing hat." I ask myself how they could strengthen their message and better engage their audience.

When I read their emails or newsletters, if I see an opportunity for improvement, I bring it up to them or save it for the future, depending on the stage of our relationship.

That's how I began my coaching and consulting business in digital marketing. I used to send my best marketing ideas to my show guests, who experienced such positive results when they implemented those ideas that they encouraged me to provide digital marketing services for others. A new business was born out of this influencer marketing strategy!

Remember, no matter how large someone's business or organization is, there's opportunity for improvement. They say, "It can always be worse." I say, "It can always be better."

Ready to pinpoint the offers that make up your unique value proposition?

Becoming aware of the value you offer will empower you to find new connections and further develop existing relationships.

Empowerment leads to confidence.

In turn, your renewed sense of confidence will help build a strong foundation for balanced relationships with influencers, where all parties respect, value, and appreciate one another.

The uniqueness of your offer

After you've defined what you offer to new and existing connections, you'll need to figure out a way to stand out, to be remembered by those connections.

But what does it mean to stand out?

People often repeat advice they've heard countless times without clearly understanding it. They say, "Differentiate yourself!" "Find what's unique about you!" "Find what sets you apart from the competition!" "Be authentic!" but they have no idea how to do that.

Those vague slogans are subject to many interpretations, so you end up confused and frustrated. I've been there! You might think you need to be "weird" or "quirky." You might wonder if you need to come up with a novel invention or a never-seen-before theory.

In my experience, differentiating yourself and your offer comes down to two key elements: focus and clear essence.

Focus

Having a "one-size-fits-all" offer makes differentiation virtually impossible.

Think about how differently a potential client or influencer connection would react to the following occupation descriptions.

Vague	Focused
I'm a marketing consultant	I help entrepreneurs tap into connections with influencers to attract the right clients and build a magnificent business
I'm a weight-loss coach	I help new moms lose the baby-weight by making a few changes to the ingredients they use in their cooking
I'm a money coach	I help recently divorced women over 55 regain control of their finances and create a secure foundation for their retirement

As you can see, focus applies to:

- The ideal client you serve

- The specific way you help that ideal client achieve what they desire

When you have a defined avatar, you can easily create a well-defined:

- Mission
- Branding and messaging
- Products and programs

Those three elements are the pillars to differentiate yourself.

When people think of me, for example, I want them to think:

- Tap into a solid network of influencer connections
- Attract the right clients
- Build a magnificent business

All of the content I create and the programs I release are aligned with that message.

My tagline, "Reveal Your Magnificence," is the essence of my mission.

If I didn't have a clearly defined target audience, it would have been very difficult, if not impossible, to articulate my mission and create successful programs.

Without a clear avatar, there's no clear offer, which will make you one of the pack instead of a standout in the eyes of new influencer connections.

That's why having a clear avatar is part of the "influencer marketing foundation" you learned earlier in this book.

Clear essence

Without a well-defined essence—a clear understanding of what you stand for—it will be very difficult, if not impossible, for you to differentiate yourself.

One of the best business books I've read is *Your One Word* by Evan Carmichael. Evan inspires readers to find that one word that reflects their essence, which can be the basis for a strong brand that stands out from the competition.

In the book, Evan says, "People want to know who you are and what you stand for before they'll buy anything from you. It's about standing for something important and having your cause be your customer's cause."[11]

Evan's "one word" is "believe," because he wants to empower entrepreneurs to believe in what they're doing, believe that they can do it, and believe that it will work. His one word became his mission statement and started his movement.

Decisions about what to say and how to say it became easy, and his brand identity was complete. Now, with more than a million subscribers on YouTube, Evan is making a difference and connecting with countless influential people.

As a side note, I had a candid conversation with Evan in which he shared a story on making the most of influencer connections, and the criteria he uses to connect with those who reach out to him with a business proposal. You may listen to the interview by visiting www.cloriskylie.com and typing Evan Carmichael in the search box.

My *one* word is *magnificent* because the essence of my mission is to help those around me realize that there's something magnificent inside them (a talent, a cause, an expertise) and to use what I teach them to share their magnificence with the world.

What about you? Do you know what you stand for and how that impacts the lives of those around you?

Once you combine your clear offer and the essence of your mission, you'll have what it takes to stand out and be remembered. Those are the key ingredients required to master your unique value proposition.

In summary, your unique value proposition is an important part of your influencer marketing foundation, and it requires a clear understanding of your offer and why that offer is worthy of being remembered.

Now, you're ready to start meeting influencers. But who should you reach out to first? Let's talk about how to select the right kind of influencer for you.

Take action!

Step 1: Write down one step you can take today to better understand the needs and wants of your ideal avatar. Will you create a survey? Post a poll on Facebook? Set up an informal chat with someone who matches the profile of your ideal client? Pick one and get to work.

Step 2: Think of one way you could make your free offer and email sequence more effective. Can you improve the content? Design? Copy? Add the mini-project to your to-do list for this week.

Step 3: Write down your unique value proposition in 50 words or less. Keep it handy as you'll need it to craft a compelling bio.

Chapter 5

The Six Success Factors to Consider When Searching for Influencers

• •

Influencer marketing principle #5: Not every influencer will be right for you—and that's okay.

• •

M aybe you've tried to connect with influencers before and got crickets instead of engagement.

Or maybe you did connect with someone with an existing audience, but the connection didn't lead to new clients. So now, you feel it will be a waste of time to try again.

You might have tried to connect with someone who just wasn't right for you and for your business.

To decide whether it's worth it to connect with a potential influencer, consider the following six success factors:

1. **Audience**

2. **Values and style**

3. **Social media following**

4. **List size and engagement**

5. **Content platform and social media engagement**

6. **The non-analytical factor**

The right connections will help you to position yourself as an authority, expand your reach, get more clients, and make a stronger impact.

Audience

Although it would be a lot of fun, I wouldn't get many new clients if I landed an appearance on Rachael Ray's daytime variety show.

But imagine how that same appearance would help my business if I were a chef or had just published a recipe book!

That's why it's not only critical that you clearly define your ideal avatar, but that you know the influencer's ideal avatar too.

If an influencer serves entrepreneurs, for example, find out what kind of entrepreneurs make up his audience before you reach out. An audience mostly made of brick-and-mortar or e-commerce businesses, for example, wouldn't be a match for you if you were trying to reach coaches and consultants.

Beware of trying to connect with celebrities with the assumption that reaching the masses will help you land new clients. It will be harder to build a relationship with a large audience that doesn't have a unifying challenge or need.

Instead, consider reaching out to those who have a smaller but much more targeted audience (niche influencers).

Values and style

A few months ago, I saw a link to a video on my Facebook feed. The post had hundreds of likes and comments, so I clicked on the link.

The person on stage was yelling at an audience member who had asked a question, with several f-bombs sprinkled throughout. Even though the speaker is an internationally-recognized Internet personality, it was clear that it wouldn't be beneficial for my business if I connected with him.

He might be very talented, entertaining, and experienced, but someone who follows him would never follow me.

Our styles are complete opposites, and that makes our ideal audiences a mismatch.

People buy from you because they feel they can relate to you. Your clients and customers like you and your style.

The influencers you connect with need to have a style and values similar to yours so that if you're introduced to their audience, you'll have the best chance to use the opportunity to grow your business.

How do you figure out the style and values of potential connections? Start by visiting the "About Me" page on their website and pay attention to their branding and message. Then, visit their social media pages and focus on the style of their posts and the content they share. You'll get a good idea of whether the person's values and style might be a good match for you or not.

Finally, keep in mind that the more you interact with an influencer, the more you will find out whether there is potential for long-term collaboration.

To go "beyond influencer marketing" means to look past one-time paid promotions or "shoutouts" commonly seen on Instagram, and instead build a long-term network of supporters and allies.

Social media following

In influencer marketing, audience size isn't the only key factor for success, but it still matters. The right influencers will have an audience large enough to potentially generate impact and revenue for you.

To make the most out of your research time, focus first on the influencer's primary social media platform. That will give you a rough idea of the size of the audience the influencer is reaching.

In most cases, there's no need to research secondary social media platforms. Don't even look at someone's Twitter account if they only have a few hundred followers there but tens of thousands on Facebook.

How do you determine the social media audience size worth considering?

I use the guidelines below to decide whether to initiate the connection or not, but I encourage you to create your own set of guidelines based on your industry. If you have to ask yourself "Is this audience large enough?" then it's probably not.

Parameters for social media following (based on the primary social media platform used by an influencer).

a. 15,000+ followers on Twitter
b. 5,000+ Facebook followers on business page or 4,000+ "friends" on personal page
c. 500+ Facebook group members
d. 1,000+ LinkedIn connections
e. 1,000+ LinkedIn group members

As prevalent as social media has become, a list of subscribers still is the most powerful way to communicate with an audience and sell products and programs.

If your potential new connection has a social media following that meets your guidelines, the next step is to learn as much as you can about their email list.

List size and engagement

List sizes are particularly important when your goal is to enter into joint venture partnerships, in which influencers will share your free and paid programs with their subscribers.

In most cases, asking people about the size of their list is like asking them how old they are or how much money they make. That's why you should never ask influencers about the size of their list and their email open rates during your initial conversation with them.

I remember a "get-to-know-each-other call" I once had with a coach interested in collaborating with me. We had spoken for about five minutes when he asked how large my list was. What I heard was, "I'm having this call for pure self-interest." His "what's-in-it-for-me" approach was a complete turn-off, and the relationship didn't go past that first call.

Now, let's say you've learned the size of someone's email list. And you didn't love the answer…

Is a partnership still worth considering?

Yes!

Someone with an audience of over 10,000 people shared one of my free downloads, and another with a list of fewer than 2,500 promoted that same download. The number of new subscribers who joined my list was roughly the same in both situations.

What made the difference was the level of engagement in each of those lists, which was evidently higher for the person with the smaller list.

You can determine engagement by comparing the open and click-through rates of your partner's list to the industry benchmarks.

A recent report on "Average Email Campaign Stats of Mailchimp Customers by Industry" shows the average unique open rates, average unique click rates, average unique soft bounces, average unique hard bounces, and average unique abuse complaint rate by industry.[12]

I trust Mailchimp because they serve companies of all sizes (from Fortune 500 companies to one-person operations). I also trust them because I've used their services for many years.

In my industry (a blend of consulting, education/training, and professional services), the average open rate for emails hovers around 21 percent, and the click-through rate around 2.5 percent.

Should you ask each potential partner what their average email open rate is? Not necessarily. If you ask this question too early in the relationship, you might make the other person wary and uncomfortable. Wait until the relationship is mature.

What if you never get this information? Then go by your experience when working with your partner. Paltry or fantastic results from a promotion will tell the whole story without having to gather any stats.

Content platform and social media engagement

You've learned that engagement is what makes a list of 20,000 subscribers with a 5 percent open rate essentially equivalent to a list of only 5,000 people with a 20 percent open rate.

Engagement is also critical in social media and content delivery platforms such as YouTube channels, podcasts, and blogs. If you can determine those rates of engagement, you can use them as an alternative benchmark to subscriber engagement.

Where do you find this information?

Go to the influencer's website and click on their blog or podcast page. Then, click on the social media icons usually found at the top or bottom of the home page. Next, pay attention to the engagement markers.

Examples of engagement markers are social media likes, shares, comments, blog post comments, YouTube channel subscribers, number of iTunes reviews, video views, and activity within their Facebook or LinkedIn groups.

There are several online tools to support your research, such as Social Blade. Even though these tools are constantly evolving, the core strategy in *Beyond Influencer Marketing* remains unchanged..

In the next section of this book, where I introduce you to the main categories of influencers, you'll learn the engagement markers per category that are most important to consider.

The non-analytical factor (gut feeling)

Once you've analyzed the values, style, and audience of an influencer, you might think you've got all you need to decide whether that influencer is a good connection for you.

But that's only half of the equation.

Imagine your best friend calls you to say she found the "perfect" date for you.

Your friend is so insistent that you agree to go on a blind date with the person.

But when you meet him or her, there's something that immediately tells you it's not a match at all.

You can't put your finger on it. You just know.

In a similar way, you've got to let your gut instinct guide you when you want to figure out if a potential connection is a "yes" or a "no."

Below are some guidelines that might make it easier for you to "read" your gut feeling.

Do you look forward to consuming their content?

If you can't wait to read the influencers' next article, receive their next email, or watch their next video, that's a sign you truly appreciate their message, and they might be a great match.

If you have to force yourself to consume the content, then ask yourself why. You know the answer…

If the reason is information overload and lack of time, you should still consider connecting with them. But if you're reluctant to consume their content because you don't enjoy it or get value out of it, that's a serious red flag.

Would you share their content even if you weren't interested in building a relationship with them?

If you'd share someone's article or podcast even if you didn't intend to build a business relationship with them, and if you're an advocate of their message because you're truly interested in letting the world know about it, the influencer is a great match.

On the other hand, if you find yourself skimming over the content and struggling to find something to say about it, that's a bad sign. Opting to write "great article" because you're not interested in reading the article falls in the same category.

Also, if you subconsciously (or consciously) minimize the impact of the share/comment and its reflection on your personal brand, that person might not be right for you.

An example of this type of behavior is to follow the influencer on Twitter, where you only have 59 followers, instead of on Facebook, where you have an audience of 7,000. Be aware of your first impulse when it's time to share someone's content or support their message, and use that as a guideline.

Do you want to be like them?

Dr. Wayne W. Dyer used to say that he only spent time with people he would want to be like. That made total sense to me! You know what they say: "We are the average of the five people we spend the most time with."

If you feel inspired by the influencers' accomplishments, and admire them for what they stand for and what they have done, that's a great sign.

However, if you wouldn't cancel your appointment with the cable guy to meet the influencer for lunch, that's a bad sign.

Holding your connections in high esteem will make it easy for you to find ways to support them, and will allow you to convey, at a subconscious level, that you're truly interested in the relationship.

Humans have about 21 facial expressions we use to communicate our feelings, and most of those expressions are subconscious.[13] Most humans can "read" facial expressions, but many can also read between the lines in text and voice messages.

If you're "not that into" the influencer, and you're reaching out for selfish reasons, your true motives will show. That will hurt your chances of making the connection and ultimately waste everybody's time.

Are you excited about the possibilities?

Finally, a good way to test your gut feeling is by using your imagination.

As an entrepreneur, you probably have an active, creative mind, and often come up with new ideas. Some of those ideas seem so brilliant to you that they turn into aha moments.

If the idea comes to you in the middle of the night, you wake up to write it down. You're so excited about your idea that you immediately put everything aside to pursue it further. You can't wait to take action to make it a reality.

That's pure excitement, one of the strongest indicators that you're on the right path.

If you feel as excited to connect with an influencer as you are when a brilliant idea comes to you, that influencer might be a perfect match.

An even stronger positive sign would be if you could clearly picture in your mind how you and the influencer would work together—down to the details.

A sense of apathy about the connection, or a vague idea of how you and your potential connection could deliver value to each other, is a sign that the person might not be the right match.

Now you're aware of the core elements to consider when making your decision to connect with an influencer.

The process isn't complete yet, though, because there are nuances that depend on the category of influencer you're considering. Next, you'll learn about the six categories of influencers and how to initiate, grow, and leverage each of those kinds of connections.

Take action!

Step 1: Write down the name of one influencer you'd like to connect with.

Step 2: Imagine the possibilities for your business if you developed a solid relationship with that influencer. Be as detailed as possible. Notice your reaction during this visualization exercise. If you don't feel pure excitement, think of another person to connect with.

Step 3: Match the person you selected with one of the influencer categories in this book, and read the corresponding chapter to learn how to create and nurture a relationship with him or her.

PART 2

THE MAIN SIX INFLUENCER CATEGORIES FOR SERVICE PROVIDERS: HOW TO SELECT THEM, HOW TO CONNECT, HOW TO SET YOURSELF UP FOR SUCCESS, AND HOW TO LEVERAGE YOUR CONNECTIONS OVER THE LONG TERM

. . . .

Depending on the kind of audience that the influencers serve and the magnitude of their reach, they'll be mass influencers or niche influencers.

The Oprahs and Tony Robbinses of the world are mass influencers, while a health coach with a Facebook group of 2,500 people is a niche influencer.

Don't dwell on whether influencers are "niche" or not. What matters most is determining if they're the right influencers for you.

To help you figure that out, I categorized influencers into six main groups. This is not an all-inclusive list, but studying these six main categories will help you learn how to tailor your approach to build the relationship depending on the influencers' medium and audience.

The six influencer categories are:

1. Podcast and YouTube hosts

2. Bloggers

3. TV show producers

4. Leaders of local groups: associations, chambers of commerce, community programs, Meetups, networking groups, library groups, and other face-to-face groups

5. Coaches or trainers leading a group, summit, or mastermind program

6. Local business owners

In the sections that follow, you'll learn how to select and connect with influencers in each category, set yourself up for success, and leverage your connections over the long term.

Keep in mind that, when I show you how to connect with a particular type of influencer, I'm assuming that you've laid out your influencer marketing foundation and that you have a clear value proposition that can be succinctly communicated to the influencer.

Chapter 6

Podcast and YouTube Hosts

....

Influencer marketing principle #6: Podcasters let you amplify your voice to extraordinary levels.

....

Connecting with podcast hosts is one of the best ways to build authority and reach large audiences. If you've created a compelling free offer for the podcast's audience, the appearance can become a powerful list-building and client attraction tool.

Best of all, once you've appeared on a podcast, you'll be able to use your interview as proof of your expertise and experience when you pitch to other podcasts.

Because Entrepreneurs on Fire with John Lee Dumas is regarded as one of the top podcasts for entrepreneurs, being a guest on the show opened doors to dozens of other interviews for me. Those appearances led to more connections and, in turn, more interviews.

Overall, podcast appearances have had an important role in the growth of my business.

If public speaking intimidates you, being interviewed on a podcast might seem a little scary at first. Don't let that stop you, however. With practice, you'll become more comfortable as a guest. If you become keenly aware of your improvement, your confidence will rise.

If after appearing on several podcasts, you still feel sick to your stomach every time you're on a show, then this medium might not be the best choice. Consider leveraging your writing or making connections with leaders of small groups. Try different avenues to share your message until you find what works best.

Six Key Questions to Ask When Choosing Podcaster Connections

Although being a guest on podcasts can be fun and rewarding, that doesn't mean that all podcasts that target your ideal audience will be right for you.

Many entrepreneurs and organizations host a podcast, but if the podcast isn't a key part of their marketing strategy, they may rely on their guests to promote the show. That won't help you significantly grow your business.

So, before you decide to connect with a podcast host, answer the following questions:

1. Is the podcast host actively promoting the show?

Check out the host's social media feeds and join his email newsletter. If a host emails his list with a summary of his interviews for the week, the show is a priority.

2. Is there a dedicated webpage for the podcast or show notes pages?

If the only place to find the podcast is on iTunes, promoting the show might not be the host's priority.

3. What's the show's ranking?

Even if a host promotes the show, a low ranking on Stitcher or iTunes might signal trouble. Do an online search for "Stitcher rankings or iTunes podcast rankings" to get an idea of the top podcasts that week.

4. Does the podcast appear in iTunes search results when you enter your ideal avatar's keyword?

If you enter your ideal avatar's keyword in the iTunes search box, and the podcast you're considering doesn't show up in the results, the podcast might not be reaching your ideal audience. For example, I usually enter "entrepreneur," "entrepreneurship," and "digital marketing" when I do my search.

Come up with two to five keywords for your search.

5. Is the show in the iTunes New and Noteworthy section?

The iTunes algorithm changes often. Also, at the time of writing this book, shows in the New and Noteworthy section hadn't changed in months. However, if the show you're targeting made it to New and Noteworthy, that's a good indicator of the effort the host has made to promote his show.

6. How many iTunes reviews does the show have?

I always check the number of reviews a podcast has on iTunes. A low number of reviews doesn't necessarily mean the show isn't good, but it might indicate that the host doesn't actively seek reviews, which goes in line with insufficient efforts to promote the show. Also, shows with a small number of reviews or sporadic reviews tend to rank lower on iTunes.

Because podcast research and selection is time-consuming, you might want to delegate or outsource the task to an assistant. I outsource the research, but I make the final decision on contacting the host.

In the Beyond Influencer Marketing bonus section, I've included a sample Excel spreadsheet you or your assistant may use to track your podcast research. Just go to **www.BeyondInfluencerMarketing. com/bonuses** to access this and all other bonuses.

Three Simple Steps to Follow When Connecting with Podcasters

Just like you, podcasters are using their show as a platform to build authority, make new connections, and grow their business. This means that they'll notice and appreciate you if you support their show. Follow these three simple steps to get started.

Step 1

The first step is to listen to the show before connecting with a podcast host. Podcasters are often approached by people who send generic emails proclaiming "I love your show," and then ask to become a guest. Other times, they're approached with specific pitch letters, but the fit isn't right. The reason for the mismatch usually is that the person who is pitching hasn't listened to the show.

If it feels like a chore to listen to the podcast, that's a sign that you might be better off reaching out to a different podcast host or a different category of influencer altogether.

Step 2

Once you've listened to a show, consider becoming an active member of the audience.

Comment on the show notes, and share your favorite episodes on social media with a customized comment on what you enjoyed the most. Always tag the host, and favor the social media platform the host is most active on. Most podcasters tend to focus on Facebook and Twitter.

Step 3

Rate and review the podcast on iTunes, and subscribe to the show, too. Ratings, reviews, and subscriptions help the podcast's ranking. Most importantly, reviews are a powerful form of social proof that will encourage new people to listen. In time, you'll become a "familiar face" in the eyes of the podcaster, which will give you an edge when it's time to pitch.

Does that mean you should never approach a podcaster and offer to be a guest on their show if you haven't completed the steps above?

No.

However, following those simple steps will help you position yourself for success, especially if the show has a large audience and receives a constant stream of pitches.

Becoming an advocate of the show will give you an extra edge, and will enhance your odds of being accepted as a guest.

The Nine Most Powerful Ways to Attract the Attention of Podcasters

How can you maximize your chances of landing a guest appearance on a podcast? This is especially important if you want to appear on high-profile podcasts and are competing against dozens or even hundreds of other guest request applications submitted in a given week.

Based on my experience, the nine most powerful ways to stand out are:

1. Invite the host of your ideal podcast to appear on your show

The process of setting up, hosting, and promoting the interview will create the foundation for a relationship with your guests.

Your guests, driven by the natural desire to reciprocate, might ask you to be on their show without your having to ask. By being on your show, the podcasters become aware of your experience and the kind of value you provide, so in many cases, they'll be compelled to invite you as a guest.

Even if the podcast hosts don't ask you to be on their show, they're still much more likely to say yes when you ask them.

2. Find a way to go the extra mile to support the show

If you don't have your own podcast, there are ways to make an extra effort to support the show you'd like to be on.

You could write a blog article about the podcast, for example, and tag the host on social media when the article is published. Be cautious when applying this strategy, however. A subpar article, a half-hearted effort to capture what's valuable about the show, or overblown praise will probably backfire.

3. Leverage what you have already done to connect with the host

If you've followed the show for a while, shared the best episodes, and posted a review of the show, it's likely that your name will be familiar to the host.

I suggest mentioning your support efforts within your pitch. For example, you could write, "Listening to John Doe's description of his struggle to grow his business in spite of his terminal disease was truly inspiring. Now, when things get tough, that message keeps me going. That's why it was such a pleasure to write a 5-star review of your show on iTunes."

Even if the host hadn't previously noticed your support, your message will bring awareness to what you've done, greatly increasing your chances of landing a guest spot. Familiarity builds trust.

4. Tailor your pitch to the host's story and the mission of the show

When I first pitched my ideas to Dave Lukas, host of the Misfit Entrepreneur Podcast, I mentioned how much I loved that he'd created the show as a legacy for his daughter.

As Dave says, "The Misfit Entrepreneur was a way for me to not only help other people on their journey, but to also have a place for my daughter to go to, long after I am gone, where she can learn from her daddy and all his Misfit friends some of the best lessons to make life richer, more fruitful, and exciting."[14]

When he learned that I related to and understood his mission, it was easy for him to agree to have me on his show.

You can do the same. Find out why they do what they do, and if it resonates with you, then center your pitch around that.

5. Offer three unique ideas for a show topic

Experienced podcasters often struggle to find fresh topics. Even if the host uses a predetermined interview format, they'll be in search of that next idea that will boost engagement.

That's where you come in.

Before I submit a pitch, I research the episodes in the past two to three months to see if anyone has explored the topics I have in mind. If my topics are fresh, I submit them. If not, I reposition my expertise with a different angle.

Let's say my topic is influencer marketing. But then I notice that only three weeks prior, another guest talked about influencer marketing as part of a business's marketing mix.

Based on that information, I pitch a different aspect of the topic, such as "how to build a list of subscribers with influencer marketing," or "how to initiate connections with social media influencers to launch your book."

Resist the temptation to speak about a topic that deviates from your core expertise. If you do that, your gift for the audience might not be relevant to the topic. Even if you create a specific download for that topic on that show, you'd have to create an entire sales funnel and email series for those new subscribers to get tangible results out of your interview.

That's why, even though I have expertise in automated sales funnels and offer funnel services, I won't speak about that topic on a show. I want to be known as someone who helps you attract the right clients through influencer marketing. Sales funnels are a small portion of the whole package.

What about you? What do you want to be known for?

I encourage you to take a moment right now and write down three to five topic ideas based on your core expertise, which you can modify depending on the targeted show.

6. Leverage common connections you have with the host

Who do you think has a better chance to get a last-minute appointment with a busy hair stylist: a complete stranger or the friend of a current customer?

The same idea applies to landing guest appearances on a podcast. Common connections matter.

Often, when I appear on a podcast, the host will offer to introduce me to other podcast hosts who might want to have me as a guest. This is one of the easiest ways to secure future guest appearances.

Other hosts may not offer a formal introduction, but instead mention shows you might like to appear on. That's what happened to me when I first appeared on the Brand Storytelling Podcast with Phoebe Chongchua.

Phoebe had been a recent guest on Evan Carmichael's YouTube show, and recommended it as a fabulous show to share my message. I followed her advice, and immediately reached out to Evan, referencing Phoebe's recommendation.

That recommendation is what allowed me to appear on Evan's show, welcome him to my show, and then incorporate the powerful lessons in *Your One Word* into my private coaching programs. Also, I introduced Phoebe to other podcast hosts and potential guests. In the end, we all ended up helping each other.

Another way to make the most of common connections you have with a podcast host is to mention that you know one or more of their previous guests.

The idea is to find common ground.

7. Send samples of previous interviews

In every podcast pitch I submit, I include links to three of my most relevant and significant podcast appearances. Those podcast interviews are relevant because they're ideal for the audience of the new podcast I'm targeting, and they're significant because they have reached large audiences.

If you haven't had podcast appearances yet, I encourage you to create audio or video clips with valuable content relevant to your audience that you publish on your site, and use those links as samples for the host.

Even though samples of actual podcast interviews are much more powerful, the mere fact that you have a sample of your work will help you stand out among the competition.

8. Craft a compelling pitch

In many situations, you'll have to send your pitch via email to the host, a contact form on the show's website, or a guest request form.

The guest request forms give you a clear structure to follow, but if you need to pitch via email or contact form, you'll love the ready-to-use podcast pitch template I created for you based on what has worked best for me in landing dozens of appearances on podcasts.

The template is part of this book's bonus package. Just go to **www.BeyondInfluencerMarketing.com/bonuses** to access the free download and all the other book bonuses.

9. Create a one-sheet

To save yourself time and effort, and to show your professionalism, I suggest you create a "one-sheet." This document is a summary of who you are and what you offer as a guest.

You could send the link to your one-sheet with your pitch, or use the information within the one-sheet to complete your guest request form or email pitch. Regardless of the situation, having this document readily available will save you time and effort.

The main elements of a one-sheet are:

1. Bio

2. Headshot

3. Potential interview topics

4. Talking points

5. Links for authority and list growth

6. Affiliate links

7. Contact information

Let's delve into each element of the one-sheet in more detail.

Bio. Create different versions of your bio (50-, 100-, 150-, and 200-word bios) so you're ready when the podcast host asks you for a specific length. If you're submitting the entire one-sheet, include the 100-word version of your bio in it.

The bio should mention your credentials and an example of the kind of results you get for your clients and customers. You should also reference media appearances, relevant accomplishments, and publications as proof of your expertise.

Headshot. It's standard for all podcast guests to submit their profile picture before they're interviewed. Invest in a professional photographer. No selfies, please!

Potential interview topics. List no more than seven topics you could explore as a guest, always ensuring that those topics are aligned with your free offer for the listeners.

Talking points. Some hosts will ask you to provide talking points for the topic you'll explore. Others favor a free-form style, and will lead the interview as an informal conversation. In either case, you should be prepared to provide talking points within 48 hours of being approved as a guest.

Links for authority and list growth. Include links to your main website, your free offer for the listeners, and your two primary social media pages.

Affiliate links. Depending on the host, you might also be asked to provide an affiliate link to a free download or low-ticket offer. In most cases, providing affiliate links isn't required, but having the ability to create such a link on demand will help you stand out. If you're submitting the one-sheet, then just write "Affiliate link for free download available."

Contact information. Include your email address and phone number.

Having your one-sheet ready will allow you to simply copy and paste the information when you complete guest request forms or pitch via email.

How to Leverage Your Connections over the Long Term

Connections with podcasters are especially powerful because of the tight-knit nature of the podcasting community and the large network of guests associated with each podcast. Let's see how those two qualities will help you.

The tight-knit nature of the podcasting community will open the door to new opportunities for you

Podcasters Paradise, led by John Lee Dumas and Kate Erickson of EOFire, is one of the top online communities for podcasters.[15] The program includes webinars, video tutorials, resources, and a

Facebook group. What members (me included) tend to appreciate the most about Podcasters Paradise is the Facebook group. Why? Because the group serves as a platform to build new connections with fellow podcasters. People join for the information and stay for the community.

Podcasters love to meet one another.

After your first few podcast appearances, doors will probably open for you. You'll have plenty of opportunities to land new appearances in front of fresh audiences.

Don't forget that the foundation of your influencer marketing strategy must be in place before you land high-profile interviews. That's how you'll be able to make the most of the opportunities.

The large network of guests interviewed by each of your podcaster connections will become your "second-degree" network

Your connection with podcast hosts will make it easier for you to connect with their previous guests, because you already have a connection in common. Many of those guests might be influencers themselves, who can lead to more introductions and a more powerful network. Your expanded network will facilitate joint venture partnerships and referral opportunities.

Don't dismiss podcasters as possible business partners. Show hosts often offer products and services that might be a good fit for your own community. By the same token, the products and services you offer might be complementary for them.

Personal Story: Unparalleled Success by Nurturing Your Influencer Network by Kate Erickson

"When John told me about his idea to launch a physical journal that would help others set and accomplish their number one goal, I wasn't sure I 'got it.'

I mean, I understood the concept, but being the implementer in our business, I couldn't immediately see all the moving pieces, let alone how they'd all eventually fit together.

As I learned more about John's idea for The Freedom Journal and how he planned to lay it out and create it, things started to become clearer.

But there was still one missing piece for me: How will we put together a communication and marketing plan that will help us successfully launch The Freedom Journal?

Turns out, John already had this figured out.

He was going to reach out to every single one of the over 1,200 guests he had hosted on the Entrepreneurs on Fire podcast and ask if they would help support our launch of The Freedom Journal.

Looking back at John's idea, it makes so much sense. John had taken the time to sit down via Skype with every single one of these individuals and help share their story on Entrepreneurs on Fire.

He had also continued to build a relationship with his past guests, one that extends far beyond the 30 minutes they shared on Skype to record the interview.

John spent the time to follow up with them when their

interview went live, and to continue to stay in touch long after their story was shared on the podcast.

In fact, many of the guests John has had on Entrepreneurs on Fire are some of our closest friends today, and that's because John took the time to reach out, offer them a platform to share their entrepreneurial journey, and cared enough to stay in touch afterwards.

With the help of hundreds of the interviewees who had shared their journey on Entrepreneurs on Fire, we launched The Freedom Journal on Kickstarter on January 4, 2016.

The result?

After 33 days, we received support from over 7,000 backers and generated over $453,000 in pledges.

We had several marketing strategies at play throughout our 33-day campaign on Kickstarter, but had it not been for the support of our network, The Freedom Journal launch would not have seen this much success."

Kate Erickson is a creator, engager, and implementer at Entrepreneurs on Fire, a seven-day-a-week podcast that interviews today's most inspiring and successful entrepreneurs. She is also the host of the podcast Kate's Take and author of *The Fire Path: A Beginner's Guide to Growing Your Online Business.* Kate is passionate about helping entrepreneurs create freedom in their business and life through developing systems and processes that can help their business scale and grow. Learn more about EOFire at www.eofire.com.

As you can see, the possibilities are limitless once you get the positive momentum going. So get started now!

Special Considerations for YouTube Hosts

I didn't place YouTube hosts under a different influencer category because the approach to connect with them and leverage the connection is very similar to that of podcast host connections.

The only significant difference between the strategy for podcast hosts and YouTube hosts is the selection criteria. Because many YouTube shows don't have an audio platform on iTunes, you should base your research on the number of subscribers, video views, and engagement on their YouTube channels.

Also, reading the comments on YouTube will give you an idea of the audience the show attracts. The words and expressions used, and the overall quality of the comments, will tell you a lot about the viewers' idiosyncrasies. It's up to you to decide if that's the kind of audience that will appreciate your message.

⤸

If you want to build connections with podcasters and YouTube show hosts, the time to start is now.

Take action!

Step 1: Write down your mission statement: "I will be a guest on _____ podcast and will create a long-lasting relationship with _____, the podcast host."

Step 2: Mark on your calendar your target date for appearing on your selected show.

Step 3: Apply what you learned in this chapter so you can achieve your goal! Don't aim for perfection. Just get going!

Chapter 7

Bloggers

....

Influencer marketing principle #7: Bloggers help you transform your writing into a vehicle to build a long-lasting legacy.

....

My first influencer connections were bloggers, and in the early stages of my online business, my blogger connections were the primary drivers of website visitors and new subscribers.

Years after publishing a series of articles on Tiny Buddha, one of the top personal development blogs, I still receive emails and comments from grateful readers.

Thanks to search engines, high-quality blog posts have a long shelf life. That's great news, because your content published on partner sites can become not only a tool for authority positioning, but a long-term source of website visitors and new subscribers.

So, if you enjoy writing and you're talented at it, prioritize making connections with bloggers and guest-posting when you design your influencer marketing strategy.

Never force yourself to write because you think you should. There are many other ways to leverage connections with influencers that don't involve writing!

When you connect with bloggers, tap into the full potential of those relationships.

A common guest-posting mistake is to view articles only as a tool for expert positioning, leaving aside the power of guest-posting as a list-building tool.

Select the topic and structure of your posts so that they naturally lead to a giveaway in exchange for the reader's email address.

For example, if your free download is "Top 10 Ways to Incorporate Avocados in Your Diet," your article could be "Seven Reasons You Need to Start Eating Avocados Today."

Analytical and Empirical Approaches for Selecting the Best Guest-Posting Opportunities

Quora listed around 150 million blogs as of 2015.[16] However, the number of active blogs on the Internet is tough to quantify, since bloggers publish new articles at different rates, and many blog owners start to write but end up abandoning their blogs.

Regardless of the exact number of blogs, the vastness of this space makes it critical to carefully select the right bloggers to approach.

Most marketers spend an average of one to two hours writing a 500-word blog post, so you want to make sure you get an adequate return on your time investment.[17]

I suggest using analytical and empirical approaches when selecting your blogger connections.

Analytical approach: Know your numbers

Numbers don't lie, so if you visit a blog that accepts guest posts with over 100 social shares and/or a minimum of 10 comments per article, it might be worth doing a comprehensive analysis.

Analyze the website data

Good research tools are Alexa and SimilarWeb. However because new tools appear and disappear every day, and many tools such as Alexa switch from free to paid, you might want to do an online search on "numbers of visitors for a website" and select the most effective tool available for your goals and budget.

Traffic rank

Let's take Tiny Buddha as an example. Looking up the site on Alexa, I see that it's ranked among the top 20,000 sites globally, and among the top 10,000 sites in the U.S.[18] That's good.

Demographics and engagement

You should also be able to see the geographical distribution of the readers (an important fact if you know where your ideal clients are), and simple engagement statistics.

Bounce rate

A website's bounce rate is the percentage of visitors who navigate away from the site after viewing only one page.

Are high bounce rates a bad sign? For blogs, high bounce rates are not necessarily negative. Readers often find articles through search engines, and once they read what they were interested in, they leave the site.

At the time I ran the search for Tiny Buddha, its bounce rate was 82 percent and the percent of readers finding articles through search engines was 42 percent—more proof the site is worth paying close attention to.

Top keywords from search engines

Use those words when you write your articles for that site to maximize the number of views for your content.

Number of sites that link to the site

The more links, the merrier, because a high number of external links helps a site rank higher in the search engines, meaning that your articles are more likely to be found.

Related sites

This is great guidance for deciding which blogger to reach out to next. For example, positivityblog.com shows as one of the top sites related to Tiny Buddha based on audience overlap. If you were in the personal development industry, positivityblog.com would be a good site to research further.

Once you've gathered the blog data, you'll have a good idea of whether connecting with the owner of the site is or isn't a wise decision.

Empirical approach: Go beyond the numbers

Selecting your blogger connections isn't only about analyzing data.

You'll also need to consider whether the essence of the brand and values of the blog are aligned with your own.

That's the key to attracting the right readers and the right clients.

Simply go through the blog, read their most popular articles, and read the "About Me" section of the site. In that section, bloggers usually tell their story and explain why they're inspired to write their blog. You'll get a sense of whether they are a match or not.

Go with your gut feeling. If you feel excited by the possibilities to post on the site, then the answer is a resonant yes.

If you feel hesitant, wait another day to revisit the site and take a fresh look at their message. If you're still hesitant, it's time to move on to the next site.

Two Ways to Improve Your Odds When Pitching to Bloggers

You could first connect with blog owners simply by pitching a guest article for their site. However, there are ways to improve your odds. As with any kind of influencer, you'll be ahead of the game if you:

- Meet them through an introduction
- Can demonstrate a track record of supporting and promoting their blog or message

We'll explore each of those situations below.

Be introduced to bloggers

Introductions and referrals are the easiest way to stand out from other guest bloggers. Once you connect with one blogger, he or she might be able to introduce you to other bloggers who reach your ideal audience.

Also, keep in mind that influencers in other categories, such as podcasters or coaches, are likely to be connected to bloggers, meaning that they can potentially make those intros as well.

To request an introduction, you must express exactly what you want. Sometimes you'll already have a mature relationship with an influencer, so you'll be able to email or call him or her directly to ask for the intro.

Other times, you'll be in the early stages of the relationship, but if the influencers ask you, "How may I support you?" be prepared to provide a specific answer. You'll miss out on opportunities if you try to "wing it." I know this because that's what I used to do.

Every time someone would ask me the question, I'd say something vague like, "Oh, well, if you know anyone who might need my services, please send them my way," which was as effective as saying "nothing, thank you." Compare that to "I want to get my article published in the Huffington Post. Do you know any of the editors or someone who could introduce me to one of the editors?"

Stand out as an advocate of your target blogger

When I started guest-posting, my goal was to promote my self-help book and messages of empowerment. That's why I sought personal development blogs.

As a consumer of books on the subject, I signed up for the Hay House Publishers blogger program (now discontinued). Members would get free access to the latest personal development books by Hay House in exchange for an honest review of the books. That was a perfect fit for me.

One day, as I reviewed the new releases, I came across Pam Grout's book *E-Squared*. The book was Pam's rendition of the *Law of Attraction*. I loved the book for two reasons. First, Pam's unique voice and stories made the reading inspiring and entertaining. Second, the book included experiments readers could try to "prove" that mastering their thoughts allows them to create their own reality, a message that resonated with me.

It was a pleasure to write the review of Pam's book, so I subscribed to her blog updates. I wrote to Pam with a link to the book review, and asked her to be a guest on my radio show. She accepted, and her interview resulted in thousands of new listeners for my show.

I became a supporter of Pam's message, sharing her books and blog with my own network, and commenting on her articles.

Naturally, when I sent Pam an article I thought would be perfect for her blog, she agreed to publish it.

At the time, Pam wasn't looking for guest bloggers. But she was willing to introduce me to her audience because she knew and trusted me.

That's how you stand out.

The way you support a blogger isn't what matters most, but the fact that you consistently support them because their message truly resonates with you. The same principle applies to building connections with all kinds of influencers.

Five Questions to Answer Before You Submit Your Pitch

Although the specific steps to get your articles published on a relevant blog will vary widely, the overall strategy to succeed with guest blogging comes down to a clear alignment between your content and the blogger's needs.

You need to know the blog and blogger so well that when you propose your idea, it's easy for them to say yes.

There are five questions you need to answer before you submit your pitch:

1. Does the blogger routinely accept guest posts?
2. Are there submission guidelines?
3. What's the preferred contact method?

4. What's the best kind of headline for this blog?

5. What is the blog post structure that best resonates with the readers?

We'll go into each of those questions in more detail.

Does the blogger routinely accept guest posts?

Although it's best to connect with bloggers who routinely post guest articles, other bloggers might still give you an opportunity to write for their audience.

In fact, many bloggers will make an exception if you build a relationship with them and offer content perfectly suited for their readers.

I was successful posting articles on Pam Grout's blog because I waited until my relationship with Pam was solid enough that she would consider my request.

I recently received an email that illustrates what not to do. I've changed a bit of the wording and the name of the sender to protect her identity.

Hello,

My name is Mary and I came across your website, which was very up-to-the-minute for me because it accepts Guest Posts. If you are still accepting them, I would be delighted to work together with you. You may feel free to look through the examples of my writing in my Google profile.

I look forward to your reply.

Mary

What do you think I did? Most bloggers would have simply ignored Mary, but I took a minute to politely say, "Thanks, but no thanks."

Mary didn't even bother to write my name in the salutation. Obviously, she sent a generic email to every website owner she could find. The email didn't even include a link to her website, ideas for articles, or samples of her writing.

I haven't published guest posts on my site for a long time now, but even if I was interested in new guest articles, I wouldn't have considered Mary's proposal seriously.

Are there submission guidelines?

If your target blog accepts guest posts, your next step is to read the submission guidelines.

Important! If there are submission guidelines, you must follow them to a T.

The first time I submitted my article to Tiny Buddha, I carefully studied the submission guidelines, and placed a check mark next to each of them before I submitted my article.

What surprised me at the time was Tiny Buddha's requirement that all paragraphs within the article be three lines or less.

As someone who was used to writing long paragraphs, it wasn't easy to adapt my writing to the blog's requirements. But I did it. And in the process, I learned the importance of writing succinct, scannable copy to increase engagement on my own blog.

Some bloggers don't want you to submit entire articles. Instead, they ask for an intro paragraph for each idea. If the site owner doesn't specify how many ideas, I suggest you submit three, which should all be aligned with the content and audience of the site.

Before you send your topics, be 100 percent sure you can write an entire article about it. What would happen if your post about "25 innovative ways to use peanut butter" was accepted and you could only come up with five ways (one of them to make a PB&J sandwich)?

What if there are no submission guidelines?

Smaller blogs usually don't have guidelines, so start by reading as many articles as you can. Look for articles related to the subject you want to write about, and pay attention to the engagement they received. Do what works!

Also, pay attention to content gaps among the articles already published that are related to your subject of expertise.

Let's say you want to write about motivation. When you do your research, you find out that the current motivation articles are about how to stay motivated during a long project and how to stay motivated after failure.

That's when you ask yourself, "What's missing?"

You could write about how to stay motivated when you get negative criticism. It's a new twist on the topic of motivation, and very likely to get a yes from the blog owner or blog administrator.

That's the process I followed to have my article published on Addicted2Success, one of the most popular success blogs.

What's their preferred contact method?

You'll usually have to submit your pitch through a submissions form or via email.

Find out the blogger's preferred submission method. Even if they have a contact form on their site, they might prefer to receive submissions via email.

If you'll be emailing your article, research whether the blogger prefers attachments, a link to the article on a shared drive, or text copied and pasted into the message itself. This is a must-do. A blogger who receives an attachment and prefers plain text will probably not even look at your submission.

What should you include in your email submission?

The answer: Exactly what's required in the submission guidelines, a short intro paragraph, and your signature. No more, no less.

Below is a sample intro for a blog that requires you to copy and paste your article within the submission email:

> *"Hi, [blogger's name], and thank you for the opportunity to write for [blog name]!*
>
> *Please see my article below as you requested on your submissions page. My bio is included at the end of this email.*
>
> *Thank you in advance for considering my article. Looking forward to hearing from you.*
>
> *Signature"*

If there are no guidelines, you may follow my guest post pitch template, which you can instantly access when you sign up for the bonus package I created for you. Just go to **www.BeyondInfluencerMarketing.com/bonuses** to access all bonuses.

No matter the submission guidelines, keep it short and snappy. Only include relevant information that will help the blogger make a decision.

What's the best kind of headline for this blog?

A compelling headline will grab the attention of the blogger or admin person in charge of reviewing guest-posting requests.

How can you come up with the most appropriate headline?

Pay attention to the favored style of your target blog, and write your headline along the same lines.

For example, if the most popular articles on a blog have "numbered headlines," such as "10 ways to cut back on sugar" or "7 strategies to boost your engagement on Facebook," a guest post with that kind of headline will have a better chance of being published.

Stay away from cutesy or cryptic headlines. Write your headline in a way that tells your readers exactly what they're going to get out of your article.

What's the blog post structure that best resonates with the readers?

As with headlines, it's best to follow the structure that has attracted the most readers, social shares, and engagement.

Following the preferred blog structure helped ensure that my articles were accepted the first time I pitched to Tiny Buddha, MindBodyGreen, Addicted2Success, and the blog of Jeff Bullas.

For Tiny Buddha, I noticed that the writer's story was always placed at the beginning of the article. Lessons drawn from the story followed, and each lesson included a reference to the main story. I followed that exact formula.

For the blog of Jeff Bullas, I noticed that the tone was much more impersonal than Tiny Buddha's. The blog's focus is on step-by-step how-to advice. That made complete sense, since it's a business blog. Unlike Tiny Buddha, where no images were required with the submission, the articles on Jeff Bullas's blog included several screenshots. I followed the formula once again and got a yes.

✢

Answering all five questions before you submit will take time and effort, but your article will have a much better chance of being accepted.

Once your first guest article is published, you'll have a writing sample to submit to other bloggers. That will significantly improve your odds of being accepted as a guest writer.

How to Leverage Your Connections over the Long Term

Even though having your article posted on a relevant blog is a powerful form of leverage, you must also nurture and foster your relationship with the owner of that blog. After all, successful influencer marketing isn't about one-off interactions, but instead about building long-term connections.

As your relationship with the blogger grows, he or she will be much more likely to post your articles, and might introduce you to other bloggers or influencers, helping you build a strong network.

Keep in mind the "value first" approach. You're contributing to the bloggers' business by creating content for them, but look for other ways to support them as well.

A few ideas to show your support for a blogger:

- Share and comment on your favorite articles published on their blog, even if they're not written by you.

- Write a positive and detailed review of the blog on its Facebook business page.

- Write a 5-star review of the blogger's book on Amazon (many bloggers are published authors).

- Recommend the bloggers and their work on LinkedIn.

There's always something you can do to stand out as a true advocate of your blogger connections.

Finally, do as much as you can to promote your guest post. Many guest writers think that their only job is to write good articles, and the promotion piece falls in the hands of the blog owners. Nothing could be further from the truth, especially if you want to make the most of the opportunity that has been given to you.

As soon as your article is posted:

- **Share it with your social media networks and list of subscribers.** When you do so, tag the blogger or the blog's social media page.

- **Reply to comments on your article every day**, especially during the first couple of weeks. You may do a manual comment check, or if the site uses the Disqus comment system, subscribe for comment notifications.

- **Provide additional value to the readers.** If appropriate, invite readers who comment to access additional resources on your site or download your free gift.

- **Consider investing in paid advertising for your article.** I usually promote my guest posts with Facebook ads, because I want to maximize the number of people who read the article, comment on it, and share it with their network. The added exposure provided by the ads will benefit the blogger and your business too. As more people become aware of what you do, your chances of gaining new customers or clients will improve.

Personal Story: Tapping into Connections with Bloggers to Grow a Multimillion-Dollar Business by Caitlin Pyle

"Back in 2011, I was fired from my job. I was devastated, embarrassed, angry—all the normal emotions one would expect to have when being unceremoniously let go from their job. But in hindsight, getting fired was the best thing that ever happened to me.

Why? Because it became the driving force behind my now multimillion-dollar business. Had I not been fired, I never would've even thought of starting my own company. But I was forced to. I took up freelance proofreading to earn income.

I did that for three years, and I did pretty well for myself: I earned more than $40k a year two years in a row. People had been asking me to teach them my ways, and while I had the knowledge to create a how-to of some kind... I had zero confidence. Who would listen to me? And who would actually pay money to learn from me? Because of that self-doubt, my first blog, Proofread Anywhere, almost never existed.

But my husband Ben encouraged me to put myself out there. So one weekend I finally wrote out an eBook on how to proofread transcripts for court reporters... and then I tried to figure out how I would get it 'out there.'

I did that by connecting with other bloggers who taught people how to work at home. I thought they might want to share information on proofreading with their audience.

And I didn't realize it at the time, but that outreach? That's influencer marketing!

Holly Hanna at The Work at Home Woman was the first

blogger to feature me on her site—even before I had an online course (all I had was the eBook at the time). I had no affiliate program; I was just a fellow work-at-home woman. When my husband found a page on her website where she said she wanted to interview women who worked at home, we wrote in, and she featured me on her blog—just like that!

I got several of my very first students that way with just my eBook. Then my gears really started turning on who else's blog I could potentially get on and how I could make it easy for them to say yes. Doing all the work for them and adding an affiliate program helped a lot.

I kept reaching out to more bloggers—and it worked! Proofread Anywhere grew to six figures within three months.

Holly and the other influencers who featured me early on are a major reason my first online course became so popular. Interviewing me on their blogs got me a lot of credibility with their audiences—and many of their audience members became my fans.

Three years, two online courses, and several eBooks and workshops later, I now get to reach back out to those influencers with an opportunity of my own via The Work-at-Home School—one of the most advanced affiliate marketing ventures ever created. And it's all because Holly gave me and my little ol' eBook a chance! That's influencer marketing at its finest."

Caitlin Pyle is a former freelance proofreader turned multimillion-dollar business owner. Her media company, BCP Media, Inc., comprises multiple brands and products that help inspire and motivate others to design the life they love.

How to Handle Rejection

What if you've connected with a blogger but your article is initially rejected?

Don't assume that once you're "friends" with the blogger, they'll publish anything you write. Your articles will still need to meet their requirements and business needs.

However, in many situations, your relationship with the blogger will allow you to get a second chance by proposing a different topic or editing the rejected article.

Ask for candid feedback and follow the blogger's suggestions. Some of the articles I wrote for Tiny Buddha went through a couple of rounds of edits before they were published.

Why did Lori Deschene, the founder of Tiny Buddha, get back to me with her suggestions? Because she knew I was an advocate of her message and a valuable contributor to her blog. That's what happens when you take the time to nurture your influencer connections.

What if your article is rejected even after editing it?

Your article could still be rejected even after making major revisions. However, that doesn't mean you've wasted your time writing the content.

Some of the topics I chose for Tiny Buddha weren't a good fit for the blog. Sometimes, Lori had already published too many articles on the topic I had chosen. When that happened, I would either edit those articles and pitch them to other sites, or publish them on my own blog. No article ever went to waste!

You, too, can use your rejected content for other blogs or your own. You can even repurpose the content and use it for your newsletter, a podcast, or a video.

∽

If blogging is your chosen medium to reach your target audience, and you're eager to connect with bloggers, take your first step today.

Take action!

Step 1: Write down your mission statement: "My article will be published on _____ blog and I will create a long-lasting relationship with _____, the blog owner."

Step 2: Mark on your calendar a target date for getting your article published on the selected blog.

Step 3: Apply what you learned in this chapter so you can achieve your goal! Don't aim for perfection—just get going!

Chapter 8

TV Show Producers

....

*Influencer marketing principle #8: People trust
in your expertise when you share it on TV.*

....

Usually, when I start talking about appearing on television shows
to grow a business, entrepreneurs tend to picture appearances
on "Good Morning America" or "The Doctor Oz Show." The
next thought that crosses their mind is, "Forget it. That's impossible!"

I would agree that it's not easy to get on shows with such broad
reach, but it's not impossible.

Let's briefly talk about how to set the stage for a future appearance
on national TV.

Two Paths to Landing a Guest Appearance on National TV

There are two clear paths you can take to land a guest appearance on
national TV:

1. A significant "new media" platform or accomplishment

2. A timely, powerful message, and a successful track record on local TV

A significant "new media" platform or accomplishment

It's become commonplace to see YouTube Show hosts, podcast hosts, and bloggers on national TV.

The reason? In two words: platform and ratings. The bigger the platform, the higher the ratings.

When YouTube show hosts and bloggers have millions of followers, they're likely to catch the attention of traditional media, including national television.

Also, national television shows often highlight New York Times bestselling authors and people who have achieved something unusual or newsworthy, such as creating a revolutionary product or service, breaking a world record, or saving someone's life.

You might not have millions of fans yet, or a bestseller, or a world record. Not a problem! Because there's another route to national television: local TV appearances.

Successful track record on local TV

Once you have several local network television segments under your belt, you'll have proven that you're a reliable and engaging guest.

So, if your products or services have broad appeal, and your ultimate goal is to appear on national TV to reach the masses, then building a successful track record on local TV might be the best way to go.

It doesn't guarantee that you'll land national TV appearances, but you'll have a way to stand out in the eyes of the producers, who are inundated with pitches from PR agencies and individuals with the next "big idea."

Consider that building a successful track record involving multiple local TV interviews will probably involve travel. The reason is that there are only a few local network shows in most cities and states.

What if national TV appearances aren't your thing?

People often ask me if being on local TV is worth it if they're not interested in building a track record to eventually be featured on national TV.

The answer is, yes!

Regardless of your future plans, television appearances offer unparalleled power to position yourself as an authority in your field.

Every time I'm on a new television segment, people tell me with a broad smile, "I saw you on TV!" My Facebook posts about new TV interviews get the most comments and likes of all.

No matter the reach of the podcast where you appear as a guest, or the blog where your articles are published, your TV appearances will appeal to people in a unique and powerful way.

And best of all, local TV appearances are much easier to secure than those on national shows.

When are you "ready" to be on local TV?

Entrepreneurs often set aside the idea of being on local TV until they're "ready." If you've had a similar thought, ask yourself why.

In many cases, your reluctance might be rooted in the idea that television is a medium for "celebrities" or those with the "right connections."

The reality is that local TV shows are as available to you as a platform for building authority and growing your business as any other option. If you use the right strategy and believe in your ability to land a local TV appearance, you'll be able to make it happen.

I've been booked for dozens of local television appearances even though I initially knew no one at the television stations and had a nascent business. You're about to learn how you can do the same.

Depending on your goals, you can use these tactics to build a successful local track record in preparation for pitching national TV shows.

How to Select Your Target Shows

If you live in the U.S., local TV shows tend to be:

1. Variety shows associated with local news broadcasts
2. Public television

Because of that, finding a show that reaches a targeted segment of the market will be tough. Exceptions might be specialized public television shows, such as a gardening show produced by the gardening club in your town.

Whenever possible, shoot for interviews at stations associated with a national network, because of the authority positioning that comes with their status.

The number of choices available to you will depend on the size of your city and state.

For example, in Connecticut, where I live, there are four choices for television appearances on local network stations (CBS, ABC, Fox, and NBC). Out of those four choices, only two (CBS and ABC) have variety shows. The other two stations bring in guests on their news broadcasts, usually to announce an upcoming event, or to contribute to a specialized segment on the weekend news.

Your next question might be, "Well, if I can't really narrow down my audience, would it be worth it to be on TV?"

The answer is a resonant yes.

Even though a large portion of those who watch your segment might not be the right clients for you, you'll be able to use your television appearance as a branding and authority-building tool.

In addition, if your topic of expertise has broad appeal, such as weight loss, parenting, or nutrition, you'll have a much better chance of reaching your ideal clients through TV appearances.

For my first television interview, my goal was to promote my online radio show and personal development book. Because my focus was on personal development, I became the expert of choice for segments on stress management, happiness, and success.

When the focus of my business changed, and I needed to reach entrepreneurs, it was a bit more challenging to come up with topics that appealed to the viewers of a daytime variety television show. But I found the connection!

I asked myself, "What segment of the viewer population might be interested in entrepreneurship, and what aspect of it might be most appealing?"

I realized that many viewers of daytime variety shows are stay-at-home moms. Those moms often wish they had a way to bring in income while having enough time to take care of their kids. The solution? A business run from home!

Then, I thought about retirees, also a big part of the viewership of daytime television. They might be looking for a new and fulfilling way to spend their time. The answer? Start a business that leverages their expertise!

I pitched my new idea: How to start a business from home with only a laptop and Internet connection. In my proposal, I mentioned how each segment of the viewership would benefit from the message. The producers loved it!

Ask yourself, "How can I 'package' my expertise into a segment geared toward the viewers of the shows in my area?" Jot down your thoughts, which will give you a head start when we explore the pitch process later in this book.

How to Connect with TV Producers

As with the other influencer categories we have explored so far, directly sending your pitch to a producer is a viable option. That's what I did to land my first few television appearances.

If you choose this route, start by finding the "Contact Us" page on the show's website. Some contact pages provide the email address for a general inbox, and others ask you to complete a contact form.

If a contact form is required, then you'll usually see a dropdown menu to select the reason for your message. "Guest appearance" will rarely be an option, but you might see something like "segment suggestion" or "programming suggestion."

Don't be discouraged by having to use a contact form or a general inbox to submit your pitch. The producers (or their assistants) are interested in new material, so they do check the submissions. If your pitch is timely and compelling, you'll hear back from them.

How can you maximize your chances of landing a TV appearance?

Look for the producer's direct email address, or at least their name, so that you can customize your message.

Where to find the contact information for TV producers

End Credits

Although mostly ignored by viewers, end credits are the most valuable source of information for finding producers' names.

Record the show and pause it as the credits roll on the screen. Write down the names of executive producers and producers, too. Local TV shows usually have one executive producer and one or two producers. Bookings might be the sole responsibility of one of the producers.

Online Search

Simply entering "X Show Executive Producer" in the search box might give you the name of the producer.

Run a new search for the name to find contact information or at least one of his or her social media pages, where you can start the connection.

LinkedIn Search

Most producers have a LinkedIn profile, and even if they're not active on the platform, they're likely to be notified when they receive an "InMail" from another LinkedIn member. InMail might be the best choice for you to reach producers directly.

If you're not a Premium LinkedIn member and don't have the option to send InMail, try sending the producers a customized invitation to connect on LinkedIn.

Personalize your invitation request and mention what you most appreciate about their show.

Once they have accepted your invitation, you can email them your pitch.

Twitter Search

Many TV producers are active on Twitter and personally check their Twitter notifications. A well-planned tweet might help you stand out among the throngs of other people pitching ideas to the show.

Get creative. Instead of sending a plain text tweet to the producer, or even an image with text and hash tags, create a short video telling the producers who you are and your ideas for the show. Also, submit your pitch via email or contact form that same day.

Remember, the more excited and passionate you seem to be, the more they'll want to know about you and the value you could potentially bring to their audience.

Referrals

If you know someone who's been on a show you're targeting, by all means, ask them for help.

If the relationship between your connection and the producers is strong, he or she could make a personal introduction (most powerful form of referral). If a personal intro isn't possible, ask for the name of the producers and their direct email addresses. When you email the producers, mention that your connection was a previous guest on the show who suggested you contact them.

How to Set Yourself Up for Success When You Submit Your Pitch

Reaching a producer is only the first step in the process of landing your appearance on TV. The next and most important step is to submit a compelling pitch.

How to come up with segment ideas to pitch

When you submit your pitch, put yourself in the shoes of the producers, who are constantly in need of interesting segments.

The never-ending search for new content is even more critical for shows that air daily. However, TV producers are often bombarded with off-target pitches.

If you can submit a suitable pitch in the most concise way, so it's quick and easy to read, you'll be setting yourself up for success.

How can you make your pitch relevant?

Just as you picture your ideal client when you create a new product or program, imagine the viewer of the show making a decision about whether to flip the channel or not. Your segment must be so compelling that the decision to keep watching becomes a no-brainer.

Seven powerful guidelines to create compelling pitches for television

Focus on local events and local talent

This strategy is applicable to local television shows, and tends to be successful because the producers are interested in promoting local talent and happenings.

You could even create a new event with the main purpose to be featured on the show. For example, if you arrange a free workshop at a local library, and the workshop has broad appeal in the area, you have a compelling reason for a pitch.

If you have recently published a book, you'll have an edge, because local TV shows usually agree to feature local authors and their new books. When you reach out to the producers, mention any awards you've received, the number of 5-star reviews the book has on Amazon, and reviews by well-known, respected authorities in your field.

Use the news

Always keep your eyes open for trends or news that the media is likely to explore.

For example, if a new computer virus that started in Ukraine weeks ago pops up in the U.S., a great segment idea would be how to keep your computer files safe. If the Zika virus is making a comeback this summer, your idea about safety tips to avoid insect bites would be a hit.

What matters is that your pitch clearly shows the link between the current event and your idea. Ideally, you'll start the pitch by briefly mentioning the relevant news.

Take advantage of upcoming holidays

Holidays are one of the easiest sources of ideas:

- Valentine's Day is the perfect occasion for marriage and relationship coaches.

- Thanksgiving is ideal for life coaches and experts on family relationships.

- Heart Health Awareness Month opens the doors to nutritionists, personal trainers, and health coaches.

Also, expand beyond traditional holidays. If you're a professional organizer, Clean Off Your Desk Day (January 9) and Clean Out Your Computer Day (February 13) represent prime opportunities for related pitches. If you're a relationship coach, take advantage of Kiss and Make Up Day (August 25). Fun and different!

Open your pitch by mentioning the holiday in question. If you're using an obscure holiday, mention when the actual holiday is celebrated and a bit of background about it.

Refer to previous segments or special themes

If a topic has been featured on the show previously, the producers are likely to be interested in ideas related to that topic.

Let's say you have a yoga studio, and a show you're interested in had a segment about meditation for stress relief. If you pitch a segment on yoga as a way to become more mindful and stress-free, you're likely to get a yes.

Also, find out if your targeted shows have themed weeks. For example, CT Style (one of the shows where I've been featured) celebrates "Wedding Week" every year. If you're a wedding planner, relationship expert, or financial planner offering financial tips for newlyweds, Wedding Week would be a perfect opportunity for you to contribute to the show.

Offer a different angle on a popular topic

If you pitch something unexpected about a popular topic, you'll be more likely to catch the attention of the show producers.

For example, a common topic on television is "Tips to save for retirement." If you, as a money coach, offer a segment on the best ways to build retirement savings based on your age bracket, you'll boost your odds of success.

When you brainstorm ideas for different spins on a given topic, think of:

- Special situations: "Gluten-free eating" becomes "Eating gluten-free while on vacation."

- Self-assessments: "Managing cravings for losing weight" becomes "What's your craving personality?"

- Current trends: "Tips for your next hotel stay" becomes "How to decide between Airbnb and a hotel?"

Offer an unusual topic

The easiest way to stand out in the eyes of the producers is by suggesting a never-explored topic that perfectly fits the preferences of their audience.

That's easier said than done, however...

Keep in mind that when the host of the show says: "And coming up..." followed by the announcement of your segment, you want viewers to either:

- Stay glued to the TV during the commercials to watch your segment.

- Resist the urge to fast-forward through your segment (if they have previously recorded the show).

Find a way to use props

TV producers *love* props. That's why I made a point to bring a prop for many of my TV appearances, even if my topic didn't seem to lend itself to a prop.

Once, I talked about how success depends on pursuing your passions. You might think that topic isn't suited for props, but there's always a way.

I built two huge paper airplanes (using 24-by-36-inch poster boards).

Using the techniques I learned when I was 9 years old, I designed one airplane to go up when I launched it, and the other to crash shortly after launching.

I used the upward-flying airplane to illustrate how someone who is following her passion will see growing success, and the crashing airplane to show what happens when we act out of obligation or pressure to follow a certain path.

That's just one example of how simple it can be to create a prop for your segment. You'll have to use a generous dose of ingenuity and creativity, but you can do it!

~§

Coming up with a brilliant segment idea is a good starting point, but it's also essential to communicate your idea with a compelling hook.

Your hook: what it is and how to use it to land TV appearances

Your hook could mean the difference between engagement and rejection. Your hook should briefly summarize your idea in a way that makes the producers want to know more.

Compelling hooks often fall into one of four categories.

1. **Social proof:** This approach is based on the assumption that if something has worked for a large group of people, or if it's endorsed by a celebrity, it might work for them, too.

2. **Move away from pain:** You appeal to people's primal fear of loss and pain. I'm not a fan of focusing on the negative, but it's human nature to be curious about how to avoid pain and suffering.

3. **Move toward result:** You highlight what your audience most wants to achieve.

4. **Case study or story:** People see themselves reflected in the story, or want to achieve similar results.

The table below features examples of each kind of hook. Apply this model to write television hooks, but also to create social media posts and even blog articles.

Social Proof	Move Away from Pain	Move Toward Result	Case Study / Story
Why 10 million Americans are closing their Facebook accounts	Facebook mistakes to avoid like the plague	Three ways to wake up rested each morning	The simple steps Amy took to lose 100 pounds
What Oprah does to beat stress	Warning: Don't drink another glass of apple juice until you do this	How to learn to play guitar in 10 days	My secret to doubling my income in less than six months
The new buzzing social media trend	Is the air in your home toxic?	Three quick and simple ways to make your kids love vegetables	How Mary got 100 new customers in 30 days

How to find the most effective pitch format

You've got a great idea for a TV segment. Now what?

As with any marketing effort, the words you choose to communicate your idea matter.

To create your pitch, consider the needs and wants of your audience (the producers). The most likely scenario is as follows:

1. They have an inbox flooded with requests to appear on the show.

2. They have limited time.

3. They're scanning their inbox for an idea worth exploring.

4. They seek entertaining, engaging guests with a proven expertise or track record.

5. They want to clearly understand what you're going to deliver when you're a guest on their show.

With that in mind, your pitch must have:

- **A compelling subject line**—the reason to open your email. That means including your hook in the subject line.

- A succinct description of **who you are and why you're an authority** in your field.

- A **clear segment idea** that matches the needs of their audience.

- A **closing remark** and best way to contact you.

I've created an easy-to-follow TV pitch template you can access as a bonus for reading this book. Just sign up for the free bonus package at **www.BeyondInfluencerMarketing.com/bonuses**. The template will help you create your first few pitches until you become comfortable writing them from scratch.

As a general guideline, your first pitch should include:

A brief reference to your credentials and expertise

Mention only the portion of your background and expertise that's relevant to the segment you're pitching. For example, if your segment is about money-saving tips for college graduates, there's no need to mention the children's book you published 10 years ago.

Include a link to your website under your signature. Alternatively, you can write, "Please learn more about me by visiting *[yourwebsite]*."

Unless you have a significant following, there's no need to include links to all your social media pages. Stick to providing only the information that will position you as someone worth having on the show.

Your idea(s)

Although you could submit only one idea, it's usually best to submit a few at a time. That way, you increase the odds that one of them will appeal to the producers.

Make sure you never waste the producers' time, though. Include multiple ideas only if they're all equally compelling.

Don't submit more than three ideas, or you run the risk of overwhelming and annoying the producers.

Links to previous television or video appearances

Producers want to know whether you have the skills and presence to be an engaging guest on TV. The best way to demonstrate this is by providing samples of your previous video appearances. Previous YouTube appearances count.

Don't overdo it with the number of samples. Include a maximum of three, and ideally select a video that features you as an expert in a topic similar to the one you're pitching for the show.

Your media reel

Once you've had more than one television interview, consider creating a media reel and adding a link to it when you submit your pitch.

A media reel is a short video compilation of the most riveting portions of your appearances. Think of it as a sampler of what you can do.

Creating a media reel doesn't have to be complicated or expensive. When I created mine, I selected my most action-packed TV segments, and then hired a specialist on media reels to create the video. You can find experienced video editors on Fiverr.com and Upwork.com.

Closing remarks and contact information

Always thank the producers for their time, and express how eager you are to contribute your skills to the show. Finally, let them know the easiest way to reach you via email and phone.

How to complete the pitch process

There's one often-neglected step that might mean the difference between landing an appearance and becoming one more pitch in the "junk pile."

That step is following up.

Because the producers are so busy, it's easy to question the usefulness of following up. Wouldn't that annoy them instead?

The fact that their inbox is overloaded makes the follow-up process even more important. Whoever makes the extra effort to check the status of their submission might be the one to stand out and be called to appear as a guest.

This doesn't mean you should inundate the producer with multiple follow-up messages. Instead, wait one to two weeks and then send a quick message to see if they received your ideas.

No reply? Then wait two to three more weeks and submit a *different* idea.

The only scenario in which I recommend not following up is when you submit your pitch through an online form, and you receive a confirmation message explicitly saying that they'll only get back to you if they're interested.

If you haven't heard from the show in two to three weeks, submit a different idea.

Now, the process is complete.

Six guidelines to help you become a regular guest

As with any influencer relationship, your mindset when connecting with TV show producers needs to be: "I'm building a long-term relationship."

Once you've been a guest on a show, it becomes much easier for you to appear on the show again.

I've landed repeat appearances on local TV shows in my state by following the guidelines below.

1. Be prolific

Although I generally advise focusing on one area of expertise as a way to differentiate yourself, you must be able to talk about more than one topic if you want to become a repeat guest on television (or podcasts, for that matter).

However, you can delve into other topics while still connecting them to your area of expertise. In my situation, if I want to be known as the go-to expert in influencer marketing, I could talk about each of the chapters in this book. If I want to appeal to a broader audience of business owners who might not be interested in influencer marketing yet, I could pitch an idea related to the influencer marketing foundation (avatar, offers, etc.) or relationship building in business.

Here's another example: If you want to be recognized as a leadership expert for women entrepreneurs, you could explore any topic related to leadership, and you could even explore the particular challenges and considerations related to being a woman in business.

2. Be engaging and entertaining

Viewers change the channel when a boring guest comes up. That's why producers will check out your previous TV or video appearances. They want to see if you're engaging and entertaining.

My #1 piece of advice is to bump up your energy to its highest level when you appear on TV or video. Even if you feel that you're going over the top, your delivery will seem natural to the viewer.

Vocal variety is essential. This includes a good mix within your pitch (using high and low notes), tone (energizing your words), volume (varying your volume for emphasis), and rate (varying your speaking rate).

What you don't want to do is to sound like a hypnotist, who deliberately uses monotone speech to put you in a trance.

If you try to memorize a script, you might panic if you can't remember the next word you were supposed to say. Relax into the conversation, and even joke around if appropriate. Listen intently to what the host is saying, so you can react appropriately and inject energy into the segment.

To make the segment more dynamic, I like to ask quick validation questions to the hosts when we're on the air. "What do you think, Ryan?" "Have you thought about that, Teresa?"

You'll be engaging and entertaining when you're being engaged and entertained. Let your true personality shine!

3. Speak in sound bites

Most television segments are short—two to five minutes on average. That's why you have to be prepared to squeeze as much as you can into those few minutes. Think in terms of short value nuggets (sound bites) rather than long monologues.

If you tend to ramble when you speak, or take over conversations, work on developing the skill of speaking in sound bites through constant practice.

As an exercise, record a mock interview in which you answer only one question. Listen to your answer, and make note of the major ideas you introduced.

Rerecord the mock interview, but this time, focus only on one major idea at a time before you stop the recording.

Next, cut unnecessary words, "ums" and "ahs," and rerecord each idea. Not easy, huh?

Repeat the process until you feel that every word you've said is necessary to convey your idea.

4. Make the producers' job easy

Especially with local shows, producers have their hands full not only with guest selection and bookings, but also with script writing. If you save them time by providing ready-to-use talking points, you'll earn bonus points.

Producers always tell me that what they appreciate most about me is how thorough I am with the talking points I submit with my pitches. "We only copy and paste," they say.

Be the guest they love to hear from.

5. Make yourself available

It's likely that when you're called to be on a show, the time suggested by the producer won't fit perfectly in your calendar. However, especially if it's your first appearance, do whatever you can (even rescheduling other appointments) to fit the interview into your schedule.

Once you've developed a relationship with the producers, requesting a different time may not be a problem, but it's still imperative that you tend to be a yes-I'll-be-there kind of guest. If you say no too many times, they'll turn to other guests who are more readily available.

If you want to go the extra mile, tell the producers you'll be available if they get a last-minute cancellation and need a guest to fill that spot. If they reach out to you for that reason, keep your word and be there!

Become a trusted resource for the producers.

6. Show you're seeking a long-term relationship

Stand out by showing your appreciation for the opportunity to appear as a guest.

A simple and inexpensive way to express gratitude is a handwritten thank-you note. The producers don't need or want another email clogging up their inbox (even if it's a thank-you email), but they'll almost always appreciate a note in the mail. Mention you're looking forward to contributing to the show again.

Finally, connect with the producers on LinkedIn. If you notice the producer is active on the platform, write a recommendation for them. Wouldn't you love it if someone did that for you? Focus on what you enjoyed the most about your interactions with the producers, the quality of the show, and the process of being a guest.

Your goal: to demonstrate with words and actions that you're an advocate of the show. With every hint of appreciation, you'll build goodwill.

Nine Proven Ways to Leverage Your Connection over the Long Term

As you already know, television appearances are one of the most powerful authority builders for an entrepreneur. However, to make the most of your interview, announcing the segment on social media or even emailing your subscribers isn't enough.

Below you'll discover how to get extra mileage out of your TV appearances. Use these guidelines as inspiration to come up with your own ideas tailored to your target audience.

1. Position your appearance as value instead of self-promotion

I once received an email from a fellow coach with the subject line "I'm on TV!" The email copy was something like "I was on X show recently. Watch the six-minute segment here."

My reaction was, "Good for you, but who cares?"

If she had instead positioned her appearance as a value-filled piece of content to benefit her subscribers, she would have exponentially increased the number of people who opened the email and watched the segment.

When you share your appearance on social media and with your subscribers, you should always ask yourself, "What is the #1 benefit a viewer will get out of this?" Your answer will lead you to the best headline and copy for your post.

2. Add a call to action during your appearance

You can use your TV appearance to directly increase your income if you add a call to action to transform viewers into customers. Examples of such calls to action are:

- Mentioning your book is now available on Amazon
- Offering a special coupon or sale for the viewers
- Announcing your upcoming paid live event

Tip: Always create a customized, easy-to-remember website address to make it as easy as possible for viewers to take action. For example, if I were going to be on CTStyle, I'd create the URL "cloriskylie.com/ctstyle."

3. Add a call to action when you share your segment, too

When you share your TV appearance, include a call to action within your post or email. This is why it's so critical to have a clear strategy in mind before you're on TV.

For example, you could invite those who watch your segment to register for a webinar that explores the topic covered on TV in much greater depth. During that webinar, you'd invite attendees to join one of your programs or purchase one of your products.

4. Build anticipation about your segment

Whether your segment is live or prerecorded, create anticipation about it on social media.

If the segment is live, announce the date and time you'll be on and the topic you'll be covering. If it's prerecorded, let your followers know the airtime.

I often share a picture of myself on set with the show hosts when I announce the date my interview will go live. I usually get fantastic engagement on that kind of post, which helps me reach more people when the show airs. For those in my audience who aren't local, I share the show's YouTube channel or website so they can watch the segment there.

5. Post your TV appearances on your website

If you want your TV appearances to have a long-lasting effect, post a screenshot of the video segment and link it to the video page on the show's website, or embed the YouTube video.

Where on your website is it best to post this video?

I suggest one of the following:

- "About Me" page
- "Recent News" page
- "Media" page

If you compile your appearances and create a media reel, post it on your home page. Excellent social proof!

6. Post your appearance on your LinkedIn profile

LinkedIn gives you an option to post links to media files, including videos, on your profile. That's the perfect virtual real estate to feature your TV interviews and attract potential clients who might want to know what you and your business are all about.

I've been approached by several people who initially learned about me through the media appearances I posted on my LinkedIn profile. The same can happen to you. However, if your ideal client doesn't "hang out" on LinkedIn, this strategy won't be the best choice for you. Deep knowledge of your avatar is a must, and a critical part of your influencer marketing foundation.

7. Create Facebook ads using screenshots of your appearances

Every time I use a screenshot of one of my media appearances in a Facebook ad, my ad's "relevance score" shoots up. Facebook advertising is beyond the scope of this book, but keep in mind that the higher an ad's relevance score is, the lower your cost per action will be. Examples of actions are link clicks, website sign-ups, likes, comments, shares, and even purchases.

The effectiveness of this strategy will depend on the purpose of your ad and your ad copy, but overall, it's worthwhile to test it against other kinds of images when you create a new ad campaign.

8. Create a media reel

Once you've accumulated more than one TV appearance (ideally three or more), you'll be ready to create a media reel to be featured on your site and social media profiles.

As I mentioned earlier, a media reel is a one- to three-minute sampler of your previous appearances, and it usually contains the most eye-catching and intriguing portions of your TV segments.

Media reels tend to be much more engaging and entertaining than a single segment, so I encourage you to create one as soon as you're able.

Use your media reel as a tool for authority building and social proof, and also as a way to maximize your chances of success when you pitch to new shows.

9. Leverage your local appearances to make the leap to national TV

Your local TV appearances can serve as a launching pad for national TV.

If that's your goal, have a professional create your media reel and submit a link to it when you pitch.

Because of the potential impact that being on national TV can have on growing your business, this way of sharing your message is definitely worth considering!

∽

As you can see, appearing on TV isn't as hard as it seems. Follow the three steps below to get the positive momentum going and make your first TV appearance happen!

Take action!

Step 1: Write down your mission statement: "I will be a guest on _____ show and will create a long-lasting relationship with _____, the show producer."

Step 2: Mark a target date on your calendar for appearing as a guest on your selected show.

Step 3: Apply what you learned in this chapter so you can achieve your goal! Don't aim for perfection. Just get going!

Chapter 9

Leaders of Local Groups: Associations, Chambers of Commerce, Community Programs, Meetups, Networking Groups, Library Groups, and Other Face-to-Face Groups

••••••••••••••••••••••••••••••••••••

Influencer marketing principle #9: Your best influencer connections might be in your own backyard.

••••••••••••••••••••••••••••••••••••

L ocal groups and associations can be one of the most powerful sources of new connections, subscribers, and referrals.

Because of their very nature, in-person interactions allow you to create trust and rapport much more rapidly than you would online.

That's why, if you can find your ideal audience at a local group or association, you should seriously consider adding this influencer category to your outreach efforts.

Three Main Factors to Consider When Selecting Groups

Since you'll need to account for driving time and meeting time, connecting with group leaders will be time-consuming. Focus your attention exclusively on near-perfect matches with true potential to drive your business forward.

I remember giving presentations through the continuing education department in my town and at the library that, although rewarding, took hours out of my schedule and didn't help me connect with new clients. I realized I needed to be much more selective.

Three main factors to consider when searching for the right group

The selection process for this influencer category is simple and intuitive. A group will be a good fit based on three main factors:

1. Current membership or audience profile

2. Audience size (total and per meeting)

3. Dynamics of each meeting

Current membership or audience profile

You must ensure that you can reach suitable clients through the group. For example, if you want to connect with life coaches, your local chamber of commerce might not be the best choice, since there will probably be only a few (if any) life coaches in the group.

To figure out who attends the meetings, visit the group's site and search for the profiles of current members (if available.) The group's "About Us" page will also give you a good idea of who belongs to the group.

Next, you can contact the leader of the group and ask directly: "How many life coaches are there in the group?" Most likely, they'll give you an idea of what to expect. If you're dealing with your local library, the librarian usually has information about the kind of people who attend their events and the audience size per event.

You might have to follow up a few times before you hear back from the group leaders, and that's okay. Be focused and persistent, especially if the group has the potential to be a good fit.

If your research and conversation with the leader tell you that a specific group might be a match, attend a meeting and see for yourself whether the group is a good fit or not.

Audience size (total and per meeting)

In my area, there are several Meetups geared to my ideal clients. However, I stay away because attendance per meeting hovers around two to five people.

Ideally, you'd want to see at least 10 attendees per meeting.

Keep in mind that the number of people who attend a meeting will often be lower than the number of people who register. You might see 15 people registered for a Meetup, but only four or five attend. The best way to find out the attendance per event (besides asking the leader of the group) is by personally joining a meeting and seeing for yourself if it's a match or not.

Dynamics of each meeting

Even though a group might seem like a good fit, it won't be unless you feel that you belong.

Here's when intuition plays a big role in your decision. If you attend a meeting and feel the impulse to check the time every 10 minutes, or dread attending the next meeting, there's no need to return.

On the other hand, if you:

- Leave the meeting feeling motivated and uplifted
- Have the impulse to immediately mark your calendar for the next meeting

Then there's a great chance you've got a match.

How to Connect with Group Leaders

As you might have guessed, the best way to connect with group leaders is in person.

Once you've selected a group or association as a promising way to reach your ideal clients, attend a meeting and introduce yourself to the leader of the group.

Make it a priority to deliver value before, during, and after the meeting. Participate, ask questions, and make suggestions. If you're an active participant, you'll soon stand out in the minds of both the leaders and participants.

I gained several clients by joining local networking groups. Even though I wasn't a speaker for the groups yet, I made a point to ask questions after every presentation, contribute my knowledge to the conversation, and share the latest marketing resources. Soon enough, people saw me as someone who "knows her stuff," and they invited me to give presentations.

Make a point to connect with the leader(s) of the group and group participants on LinkedIn or Facebook, and keep notes on what stood out about your conversation with each person. Did they mention their cockapoo? Did they talk about their love of pomegranate juice? Paying attention to details will help you build rapport and nurture your new connections.

How to Approach Formal and Informal Groups

Your strategy will depend on the kind of group you're considering. There are two broad kinds of groups:

1. **Private groups with informal structure**, usually led by one person or a small group of people (Meetups, networking groups, some chambers of commerce, etc.)

2. **Organizations with a formalized structure**, which often have ties to the local government (libraries, continuing education departments, etc.)

Private groups with informal structure

When it comes to private groups with an informal structure, you might meet your ideal clients simply by participating in the right groups. However, in influencer marketing, your goal is to go beyond basic one-to-one networking and to be introduced as an expert in your field.

When should you ask if they'd like to have you as a speaker or contributor to the group?

You'll be able to tell when your relationship with the leader has reached (or is nearing) a point of maturity. The leader will know you by name, and ideally will have offered positive feedback about your participation in the group. That's when you can propose your idea for a presentation.

Unsure if it's the right time to ask? That's a sign you'd better wait.

Organizations with a formalized structure

If you're dealing with an organization such as a library or continuing education department in your town, the process may be a little more involved. They're likely to ask you to submit a speaker request form.

In general, you won't need to have the same kind of close relationship you'd want with the leader of a Meetup or networking group.

Creating a proposal for your presentation

Whether the group has a formalized structure or not, you'll probably have to create a proposal for your presentation.

Your proposal can be a simple one- to two-page document that includes:

- Title of the presentation or class
- Summary of the topic and the main result attendees will gain (no more than 100 words)
- Three to seven bullet points with the main talking points or lessons to be covered
- Your 50- to 100-word bio and qualifications

Apply the same strategy you'd use to create a webinar registration page. Your copy should be results-oriented, and the title (headline) must be attention-grabbing. Make it a no-brainer for people to invest their precious time attending your event and listening to what you have to say.

Submit your proposal in person or via email, and follow up in a week or two if you haven't heard from the leader of the group. In your second message, propose a different topic if the original isn't a good fit for the group.

In these kinds of organizations, decisions can take a long time. I had given up on a group presentation after three follow-ups and no response. Two months later, I received an email with an apology for the late reply and an invitation to meet in person to talk about my proposal.

Five Strategies for Building Authority and Growing Your List with In-Person Presentations

Let's say you've sent your proposal and you got a yes. It's not time for the champagne toast just yet. To make your presentation worthwhile, you'll need to ensure that it serves as a vehicle to build authority and gain new subscribers.

Here are the strategies I've used in my business and recommend as some of the most effective for in-person presentations.

Five strategies for building authority and growing your list with in-person presentations

1. Write your own introduction

I've attended presentations where the speaker introduction was so brief I wasn't sure why I should be listening to him, and others where the introduction dragged on for so long that I was ready to go before the presentation even started. The best way to avoid those situations is by writing your own introduction.

Write a bio that gets your audience excited and interested in what you have to offer. Go beyond degrees and titles. Add related publications, appearances, and other tidbits of unique (even a bit quirky) information that will make you stand out.

You might already know many of the group members who attend your presentation, but you'll meet new people that day, too, so write your intro with those new people in mind.

If your presentation is hosted by an organization such as a library or continuing education department, then almost everyone won't know who you are, which makes a compelling bio even more critical.

Answer the following questions about your audience to help write your introduction.

What is the main result they want to get and how do my qualifications help them get those results?

- What do they value most?

- Why should they care about what I have to say?

- What publications or certifications are they familiar with?

- What objections are they likely to have about my topic or my level of expertise?

- What is my core mission? How do I express my mission in a memorable and relatable way?

- Can I make a connection with them by tossing in something personal about me?

2. Record your presentation

Recording your presentation has two powerful benefits:

1. Watching the presentation from the perspective of your audience will help you make your next presentation better.

2. You'll be able to use the recording as a resource to gain new subscribers and clients.

I'll explain the second benefit in more detail.

In exchange for a link to the recording of your presentation, you'll ask the attendees for their email addresses.

Come to the meeting prepared with a sign-up sheet or a set of contact cards. Alternatively, you could give them a number to text you their email address. Make your request *before* you end the presentation, when you have people's undivided attention.

Be clear that, by providing their email address, attendees will be added to your mailing list and will receive future communications and resources from you. Setting clear expectations from the start is a must. You don't want to be labeled as a spammer!

Also, you could use the recording as a lead magnet or as a bonus for one of your paid programs. You could even sell it as a stand-alone product, but keep in mind this might require permission from the organizer.

The quality of the recording must be as high as that of your digital programs, so it's essential to hire a professional videographer. I made a costly mistake when I hired a "bargain" videographer. The final recording of my presentation was of such low quality that it was unusable, so I ended up wasting my time and money.

3. Distribute feedback forms

Even if you're an experienced public speaker, there's always room for learning and growth. Also, there will always be new ways to make your presentation more compelling. That's why feedback forms are essential.

Distribute the forms when you wrap up your presentation, and explain why your attendees' input will help you create better presentations for their future benefit. Remember, it's always about them, not about you.

In the feedback form, ask about attendees' level of satisfaction with:

- **The content of the presentation** (clarity, quality, use of stories or case studies, relevance)
- **The structure of the presentation** (logical flow, transitions, length)
- **The technology/visual aids** used (effectiveness, appeal)

- **Your delivery** (engagement, body language, voice, skill level to answer questions)

To make it easier for the attendees to provide their feedback, use a rating system to gather the information. For example, use a scale of 1-5, where 1 is most dissatisfied and 5 is most satisfied.

Include space for additional comments. End with an invitation to enter their contact information in exchange for a related resource from you, such as the video recording of the presentation. That's another opportunity for you to build your list with this highly targeted audience.

4. Offer a compelling way for attendees to join your list of subscribers

We've already mentioned offering the recording of the presentation in exchange for the attendees' email addresses, and asking for their contact information on the feedback form.

You could also show a presentation slide with the phone number where attendees can text you their email address, and leverage a text capture service to automatically send them the resources.

What else could you offer to capture email addresses?

- PDF version of your slides
- Workbook
- Webinar to explore the topic in more detail
- Cheat sheet with a summary of the presentation
- List of resources shared during the presentation
- Video training series on the topic

Always make clear that everyone who provides their email address will receive regular updates and resources from you.

5. Use your audience's questions to come up with new ideas for future presentations

Finally, your presentations can serve as a springboard to create new presentations and products. The attendees' questions will provide useful feedback about the knowledge gaps within your ideal audience. Guess who's going to be there to fill those gaps? You, of course!

So, another benefit of recording your presentation is that you'll have a way to review and analyze the questions at a later date (rather than relying on memory alone).

Instead of just answering questions, ask your own follow-up questions to those who participate.

For example, let's say your presentation is about how to run Facebook ads and someone asks you whether video ads tend to be more effective than "carousel" ads.

That's your opportunity to ask what kinds of ads they have tried in the past and what purpose those ads served. If the person says they're using the ads to boost their Facebook followers, you'll know that a presentation about how to grow one's following on Facebook would be well received.

Bottom line: The point is to make the most of your presentation and the extensive amount of preparation associated with speaking in a face-to-face meeting.

Once you have a winning presentation, all you'll need to do is find new audiences who might be a good fit for your message.

There's nothing like being face-to-face with your ideal clients to create a strong connection and receive instant feedback about your message.

Also, local leaders can become advocates of your business and help you stand out online and offline. I encourage you to consider connecting with leaders of local groups as part of your influencer marketing efforts.

Take action!

Step 1: Write down your mission statement: "I will be a guest speaker at _____ and will create a long-lasting relationship with _____, the group leader."

Step 2: Mark a target date on your calendar for appearing as a guest speaker.

Step 3: Apply what you learned in this chapter so you can achieve your goal! Don't aim for perfection. Just get going!

Chapter 10

Coaches or Trainers Leading a Group, Summit, or Mastermind Program

....

Influencer marketing principle #10: The fast-growing coaching and training industry expands your options to connect with influencers.

....

The coaching industry is rapidly growing, and with that growth comes new opportunities to connect with entrepreneurs who lead a group coaching program, mastermind, online summit, or live event. In many cases, you'll be introduced to an audience of paying customers, who are much more likely to invest in new products and programs (including yours).

If you're a speaker on a virtual summit, then not all members of the audience will be paying customers, but many of them will be. Also, summit participants often receive a great deal of valuable training at no cost, which creates a significant level of goodwill. That goodwill leads to an increased willingness to join your list and sign up for your products and programs.

When you collaborate with coaches or trainers, you'll usually agree on a revenue share or affiliate commission. We'll talk about this in more detail later in this section.

Three Critical Factors for Selecting Your Connections

As with other influencer categories, not all coaches and trainers will be ideal matches for you.

There are three critical factors in the vetting process:

1. Audience
2. Values and style
3. Offers

Audience

To start, you need to learn all relevant details of the audience the coaches and trainers serve. Never skip this step, or you may be in for an ugly surprise.

For example, many business coaches only serve "heart-based" entrepreneurs, also called "spiritual" or "conscious" entrepreneurs. Those entrepreneurs often prioritize impact over profit, so if your message is centered on profit maximization, you may have a hard time creating a connection with the audience.

Here are sources of secondary research to find more about the audience of the coach or trainer you intend to reach.

Website and social media search

You'll find a substantial amount of information on their About Me pages and social media pages. If the influencers are active on LinkedIn, they might describe who their ideal customers are in their profile description.

Third-party market intelligence solution

I love using a tool such as SimilarWeb.com, where I can find business data not available on the influencers' websites and social media pages, such as:

- Countries they reach
- Website traffic sources
- Keywords
- Most relevant social media platform
- Competitors and similar sites

Content platform

You'll find great information on their blogs, podcast show notes, YouTube channels, and any other content platform they use.

Pay attention to the comments. People who comment the most tend to reflect the core audience's values, style, and preferences.

Groups

You'll also be able to learn about your potential connections by joining their Facebook or LinkedIn groups. Pay attention to the most active group members, who are likely to fit the ideal client profile.

If the audience is a good match, then you can consider the next success factor: a match between your values and style, and those of the influencer.

Values and style

Think about this: What makes you relate to a book, movie, or show? Isn't it all about feeling that they "get you"? Maybe you find yourself nodding in agreement, laughing at the jokes, or thinking, "yes, me too!"

This part of the equation might sound like plain intuition... because it is!

Start by watching the influencers' videos, listening to their interviews, and reading their blog posts.

Initiate the connection only if you say yes to all the following questions:

- Does their message resonate with you?

- Do you feel compelled to consume more of their content?

- Do you want to learn more about their entrepreneurial journey?

- Would you feel good if you shared their content with your audience?

If you answered no to any of the questions above, it might be best to move on. Remember that your connection will ideally become a long-term business partner or even a friend, and you don't want to hang out with someone you can't relate to, right?

Offers

Finally, you should aim to connect with indirect competitors (those who offer complementary products or services). It's unlikely that a direct competitor will want to introduce you to their audience. Also, indirect competitors offer the greatest opportunities to create joint programs and cross-promotions.

Move forward with the outreach process only after you've confirmed that there's a clear match with the influencer's audience, values, style, and offers.

Four Proven Ways to Connect with Coaches and Trainers

There are four powerful ways to connect with coaches or trainers:

1. Joining one of their paid programs
2. Participating in the same program or association
3. Meeting them at a conference or event
4. Supporting their message online

Joining one of their paid programs

Let's say you're trying to dig out of your email pile. Which message would you click on first: the one from a new customer or the one from a stranger?

That's how most coaches and trainers feel...

Once you join the influencers' programs, you'll immediately gain their attention, and depending on the program, you may have access to their private Facebook group, live group meetings, live events, and even private sessions with them.

But joining the programs alone isn't enough to grow the connection. Become an active participant by asking questions during group meetings, posting comments and questions on their private Facebook group, and offering support to fellow participants in the program.

Once you complete their program, the best way to continue to stand out is by offering a testimonial that includes the results you've achieved with their training.

Written testimonials are always welcome, but video testimonials are more powerful. All you need is a minute of your time and your phone!

Participating in the same program or association

If you've joined a training program with a Facebook community and someone in the program invites you to connect, would you accept?

In most cases, your answer will be yes. Simply being in the same program creates a sense of trust.

The most valuable part of many of the programs I've joined isn't the training I received, but the connections I made with fellow participants.

I've met most of my business partners through training programs such as JV Insider Circle, a top community to master joint venture collaboration. As my relationship with the leaders of the program deepened, I was invited to join the team in a formal coaching role, an invaluable opportunity to strengthen my positioning as an expert in digital marketing.

Associations have a similar effect to that of paid programs. When someone feels you're both members of the same community, they tend to trust you, and they're more likely to want to get to know you.

Meeting them at a conference or event

Have you stayed in touch with people you met at an event?

There's nothing like face-to-face interaction to create camaraderie and initiate a connection. Try to make room in your schedule and budget for at least one conference per year.

You can supplement your attendance at large events with participation in smaller events in your area. Research local Meetup and networking groups where coaches and trainers are likely to be. Apply the strategies we covered under the "Leaders of Local Groups" section earlier in this book to find meetings that promise to be a good fit.

Supporting their message online

As you learned earlier in the book, the main idea is to become an advocate of the influencers' message by commenting on their posts and sharing them with your network.

This also involves sharing their blog articles, podcasts, and other content on social media networks, along with insightful comments that add value to the content.

How to Set Yourself Up for Success When You Approach Coaches and Trainers

Regardless of how you meet the coaches or trainers, always approach them with the value-first mindset that we've explored throughout this book.

Connecting with someone with self-interest in mind isn't likely to lead to a long-lasting and beneficial relationship. **Focusing on value first is what you do when you go "beyond" influencer marketing.**

Along the same lines, don't give in to the temptation to ask for support from the coach or trainer too early in the relationship.

Often, I've been approached by fellow coaches who in the first 10 minutes of our first phone conversation ask me if I could promote their products to my subscribers. Then, without listening to my reply, they announce: "You'll make a 30 percent commission!"

Other times, coaches invite me to "friend" them on Facebook after we've interacted on a Facebook post. Then, when I accept their request, they type in Messenger: "Nice to connect. What are you working on?" or "Nice to connect. How may I serve you?" And then, ignoring my answer to their question, ask me if I want to jump on a call to talk about their upcoming product launch.

Those coaches don't realize they've just made two rookie influencer marketing mistakes: prioritizing their own gain and assuming that I'll be interested in promoting them solely because of the commission.

Those mistakes are much worse when you don't even have an existing relationship with the influencers.

Most coaches and trainers will agree to collaborate with you because they trust you and feel your product or program will be of value to their audience. They're aware that anything they promote (including your offers) will reflect on them and their personal brand.

Rookie mistakes could ruin your relationship before it even starts.

When we explore the three stages of influencer relationships, you'll learn how to recognize when your relationship has grown to a solid-enough point to propose your idea for collaboration. For now, a good gauge to know if it's the right time to pitch is how you feel as you contemplate the idea. If you feel uneasy or doubtful, it's probably not the right time.

Three Key Ways to Collaborate with Coaches and Trainers: The Road to Joint-Venture Partnerships

Your imagination is the only limit to the ways you can collaborate with coaches or trainers. Let's explore the most common and proven options to work with them.

- Interviews
- Presentations to customers or clients
- Joint venture promotions
  - Joint webinars
  - Product launches
  - Group giveaways

- Summits

- Referrals and intros

Regardless of the form of collaboration you end up choosing, keep in mind that the number one goal of the alliance is to deliver value to the audience. Sales pitches without value added will not only be a turnoff for the audience, but will also permanently damage your relationship with the coach or trainer.

Also, in every situation, find a way to reciprocate. If your list of subscribers is too small for an email campaign to have a significant impact, extend an invitation to the coach or trainer to give a presentation to your clients or customers (highest qualified audience). If you have thousands of subscribers, you can leverage your list to promote your partner. Continuously deliver value to your connections.

Interviews

Interviews represent an "entry-level" collaboration with a coach or trainer. There's a great deal of value delivered, and usually nothing for sale.

That's why it's usually a good idea to ask if you could be a guest on the coach's podcast, YouTube channel, Facebook group, or blog.

If that still seems like too much, then start by interviewing them, or suggest a "guest swap."

Video interviews are fantastic because you can repurpose the transcript as a blog post, and use snippets as social media content. Also, as new livestreaming apps pop up, it's increasingly easy to "go live" with your guest. I did a short series of 10-minute live interviews with some of my closest connections, which I now use as valuable content for my new subscribers.

Blog interviews are another option. However, beware of giving answers that lack step-by-step guidance. Always add actionable steps when you answer the questions, as though you were writing a blog post.

Once you've been a guest, it will be easier for you to participate in future interviews. One of my colleagues invited me to participate in a "collaboration post," in which a handful of selected coaches wrote about how they connected with their first client. The article, which received thousands of views, provided great exposure for my business, and it helped my colleague build authority as the person who gathered and analyzed all the expert responses. She also benefited from the shares and comments from the participants in the post.

To succeed with podcasts and YouTube interviews hosted by coaches or trainers, use the guidelines for podcast interviews we explored earlier in the book. Remember, you must be prepared with a giveaway to build your list, and with a clear customer journey for your new subscribers.

Presentations to your contact's customers or clients

Many coaches and trainers offer group training, coaching programs, retreats, or masterminds. Such programs tend to require a significant investment of time and money from the participants. Because those participants have proven that they're willing to invest in themselves, they're ideal potential clients for you.

Coaches and trainers will tend to be more guarded about bringing guest speakers to their paid programs, so you must build a strong relationship with them before suggesting this kind of collaboration.

Ideally, you'll propose a presentation that complements your contact's program. At the end of your presentation, some participants will want to work with you to implement the strategies you discussed. If that's the case, then it's best practice to share a portion of the revenue with your contact. Some coaches and trainers might not be interested in a revenue-share agreement but purely in the value you add to their program. That's why you and your new partner will need to lay out the specifics of your collaboration from the start.

Well in advance, share with your connections the two key offerings you're planning for their audience:

- A giveaway to collect email addresses
- Your paid offer and the special discount or bonus for event participants

After the event, your connections should feel they made a fantastic decision by working with you.

Joint venture promotions

Joint venture promotions are partnerships, so they often require a mature business relationship or at least a deep level of trust from the partner who's participating in the promotion. Most people will want to know exactly what your offer entails before they agree to work with you. They might even require testing your offer before they make a decision.

Affiliates versus joint venture partners

I'm often asked what the difference is between affiliates and joint venture partners. The main gap lies in the level of commitment and strength of the relationship between the parties.

For example, a blogger might include within her blog posts Amazon affiliate links for books, supplements, or tech gadgets in hopes of adding revenue, but she'll probably never know the creators of the products being promoted, or try to create a relationship with them.

In contrast, joint venture partners aim to collaborate not only because they want to increase their revenue and value delivered to their audience, but because they believe in each other's message and want to help each other. Joint venture partners provide a level of support and commitment well above that of an affiliate partner.

When you build a relationship with a coach or trainer, you'll be paving the way for a joint venture relationship.

Components of joint venture partnerships

There are two main components of joint venture partnerships:

- Value
- Revenue share

Value

Would you agree to promote a subpar event, even if you were offered a 100 percent commission?

No way, right?

Nonetheless, entrepreneurs who are new to JV partnerships often think that the revenue share is what's most coveted by their potential partners.

Don't make that mistake.

To committed coaches or trainers, their audience is their biggest asset. The last thing they'll want to do is to jeopardize that asset by bringing in someone who doesn't offer a product or program that is at least of the same quality as their own.

I've received emails that say, "I've got an amazing program for entrepreneurs for you to promote. I'm offering 40 percent commission on the $997 level, which means almost $400 per sign-up! Do you want to book a time to chat?" They don't even explain the benefits of the program. Ugh. No thanks.

How do you ensure your offer is perceived as valuable?

Your offer must be:

- Able to achieve the results you claim (as shown through testimonials)

- Complementary to what your potential partner offers (narrow scope). For example, if your potential partner is a career coach who provides job search services, your LinkedIn program might be a perfect fit. However, if you offered an A-Z guide to finding a new job, you'd probably be out of luck.

Revenue

If you're confident that your offer is of value, you can focus on the revenue share you'll offer to your partners.

I was once offered a 10 percent revenue share on a $197 program. What do you think I did?

Consider this:

- A generous share of the revenue will incentivize the coach or trainer to promote your program.

- A paltry share of the revenue might jeopardize the joint venture relationship.

What's the customary revenue share for businesses in the "experts industry" (coaches, consultants, trainers, speakers, practitioners)?

It's customary to share 30-50 percent of the revenue generated by digital training and group programs.

For low-cost offers such as books or inexpensive training programs, the revenue share can be as high as 100 percent. In that case, it's common to offer a 20-50 percent commission on the upsells (higher-priced offers) for those who have purchased the inexpensive product.

For more expensive services or programs, you can expect to share anywhere from 5 to 20 percent of the revenue generated by your partners. In many cases, you can offer a lump-sum gift for new clients or customers.

Carefully study what the unspoken rules are for your particular industry, and abide by that.

The tech side of joint venture partnerships

Having a sound technology platform is essential for joint venture partnerships to be successful. Besides having a highly converting landing page for your free offer and a valuable free offer, you'll also need software to track the referrals from each partner.

If you don't have a tracking system, your partners will have to take your word that you're tracking sales correctly. The trust system leaves too much room for error, so I suggest implementing a reliable affiliate tracking system from day one. There are many technology platforms to choose from, with new tools being developed every day, so I won't recommend a specific tool.

It's essential to choose a user-friendly tracking tool with readily available stats in a secure affiliate area.

I once agreed to promote someone's product, but I was never granted access to the affiliate site. Instead, I was sent a tracking link. I decided to accept the "trust system," but my partner never sent me updates on how many clicks, opt-ins, and sales I was generating throughout and after the promotion. I received no reply to my multiple follow-ups. Needless to say, I lost trust in that person and the relationship fizzled.

Communicating with and rewarding your partners

Regardless of the commission you offer and the technology platform you choose, you must clearly communicate the terms of your business relationship with your partners, and honor your commitments. That means sending accurate and timely payments. In the experts industry, it's common to submit commissions at the end of a program's refund period.

I've agreed to promote many entrepreneurs, and unfortunately, I've ended up regretting many of those partnerships. The root cause of all the mishaps was poor communication and broken promises.

Remember that you're building long-term relationships, and a single promotion gone wrong can jeopardize the whole relationship. Also, word about who the good and bad partners are spreads fast within an industry. Do what it takes to keep your personal brand and reputation strong.

Five ways to run joint venture promotions

In this section, you'll learn five ways you can run a joint venture promotion, particularly if you have a service-based business. Use your creativity to come up with new ways to collaborate with your partners that deliver the most value to their audience.

1. Joint webinars

On a joint webinar, your partner is the host of the event and you're the special guest. Your partner usually moderates the webinar, too. The presentation is customized to the needs of your partner's audience.

If you choose this route, create a free offer that's simple and easy to consume, such as an eBook, a PDF guide, or a checklist. You can use that resource as a precursor to the webinar invitation. The benefits of this approach, rather than sending people directly to register for your webinar, are:

- You'll build trust with the audience from the get-go. No need to attend your webinar to figure out if you have value to offer.

- You're likely to get a higher subscriber rate. A quick download represents a much lower level of commitment than a 60- to 90-minute webinar presentation, so people will be more inclined to opt-in. Once they've joined your list of subscribers, you'll be able to continue communicating with them even if they don't attend your webinar.

When you host a joint webinar, your partner will email their subscribers with a link to your free offer and webinar registration link. I suggest sending a total of three messages to the list with two or three days between messages.

Keep in mind that, although it's most effective if your partner writes his or her own email copy, you'll be expected to provide "swipe" copy (ready-to-use text for the email campaign).

Caveat: It's a numbers game…

Coaches and trainers with audiences of less than 5,000 subscribers might not be able to attract enough participants to your live webinar to make it worth your and your partner's time. This is closely tied to engagement among the subscribers, too.

I once participated in a joint live webinar with a partner who had a few thousand subscribers and low level of engagement. Only 32 people registered, but we still went ahead with the live presentation.

We were in for a disappointing afternoon when no one showed up for the webinar. In retrospect, a prerecorded webinar would have been most appropriate.

2. Product launches

In a product launch, you'll build anticipation about the release of your product or program. Apple is a master of product launches. Their carefully crafted campaigns capture the attention of millions. You've seen the results: Thousands of customers camp out, sometimes in freezing weather, so they can be one of the first to lay hands on the new iPhone.

In the expert and service industries, Jeff Walker has become a "Product Launch Guru." In his book *Launch*, Walker explains how his marketing model works. To drive sales, he offers what he calls the sideways sales letter, which "is a sequence of Prelaunch Content, followed by a sales message. The typical sequence will have three pieces of Prelaunch Content, which you share with your prospects over a period of up to 12 days."[19] The objective is to deliver value and build momentum for when the product is available for purchase. In Walker's model, the product is usually available only for a limited time (until "cart-close" day.)

Regardless of the model you select to launch your product or program, your joint venture partners will promote your free content and paid offer, which must be of the highest quality for the success of the launch.

Selecting your launch date

When you select your launch date, keep in mind that you'll need to give your potential partners enough notice to fit your campaign into their promo calendar. For most coaches and trainers, a six-month notice is best, although some might require as much as a year's notice.

If your partner doesn't routinely incorporate JV campaigns into his or her schedule, then a shorter notice might be okay. Bring this up during your initial JV partnership conversations. Ask them how many partner offers they usually promote in a year and how far in advance they plan their promotions.

Communicating with your partners

Also, during the prelaunch and launch periods, you'll be campaigning to your audience and to your partners. It's critical that you stay in constant communication with all parties if you want them to remain engaged during the launch. People are busy, so your launch is not their priority.

That's why you should prepare to run two launches simultaneously: one for your potential clients and one for your partners.

When I've done product launches, I usually send out:

- An email to partners eight weeks prior to the prelaunch

- A reminder email four weeks out

- A second reminder a week prior

- Daily emails starting a day before the prelaunch through the end of the launch (cart-close)

I encourage you to think of creative ways to engage your JV partners. When I promoted "Magnetize Your Audience" by Justin Livingston and Callan Rush, I received a thank-you note and a box of whoopie pies a week before prelaunch. That small but very nice gesture made me even more excited to promote their program.

Once your launch is complete, I suggest hosting either a private call with each partner or a debrief meeting with all partners. Share what worked well, what didn't, and lessons learned. Your goal, once again, is to provide as many insights as possible to your partners and to lay a solid foundation for future JV promotions.

Explaining the ins and outs of product launches is beyond the scope of this book. However, I recommend Jeff Walker's book *Launch* as a good resource to learn more about this strategy to sell your products and programs.

3. Group giveaways

Group giveaways can help you grow your list. In a giveaway, a group of entrepreneurs contributes a free offer. All free offers are bundled and made available in exchange for people's email addresses.

To create scarcity, giveaways are only available during a limited period (usually a week or two). In most cases, participants are offered a paid product after they access their gifts.

Organizers of group giveaways have a huge advantage, because they gather all of the participants' email addresses through a master opt-in page. The rest of the entrepreneurs participating in the giveaway only capture the information of those who decide to opt-in for their free offer.

When you're the leader of the giveaway

Group giveaways have been overused in the past few years, so they've lost effectiveness. However, you'll be able to build your list significantly with this strategy if the gifts in the giveaway offer tangible value rather than being a bundle of disguised sales pitches and sneaky ways to make people buy the participants' products.

If you host a giveaway, you'll be helping your partners build their lists—a great way to build trust and goodwill for future partnerships.

The best giveaways offer clear outcomes for specific audiences. A "Success Giveaway" is ironically destined to be less successful than a "List-Building for Coaches" giveaway.

As with any form of collaboration, you'll need to create top-quality landing pages, email campaigns, and social media promotions to invite people to the giveaway.

Also, when you pitch your idea to your potential partners, you must clearly convey its value for their audience and for their business.

What your potential partners will care about most is:

- **Other contributors in the giveaway**. What do they offer? What's the size of their business? What's their average list size? Those factors will impact the personal brand of the contributors, and the number of subscribers that each person gains.

- **Promotional needs for the giveaway**. How many times and how often will they need to promote the event?

- **Giveaway schedule**. What are the beginning and ending dates of the giveaway? Early notice is best so that contributors can fit the promotion in their calendar.

- **Resources provided for the participants**. Will they have access to swipe copy for email and social media campaigns? Will you also provide images for the promotion?

Once your giveaway is complete, hold a debrief call or meeting with your partners. Just as you would after a launch, share your insights from the process and plans for future giveaways.

Finally, gather the partners' feedback on the giveaway and the results they achieved. If your first giveaway resulted in an average of 1,000 new subscribers per participant, for example, you can use those stats to pitch future giveaways to new partners.

When you plan to be a guest contributor for a giveaway

If you connect with a coach or trainer who regularly hosts giveaways, mention your interest in participating well in advance of their next scheduled giveaway. Worst-case scenario? They say no. So what?

At least you gave yourself a chance, and they might invite you in the future.

Also, put yourself in your partner's shoes, and create the kind of offer and promotional campaign you'd love to get from contributors if you were the host. Your list might include:

- A high-quality free offer with tangible value tailored to the audience
- A well-crafted email sequence for new subscribers
- A strategy to promote the event as much as possible

Once the giveaway is complete, follow up with your partner to thank him or her for the opportunity. Offer your insights about the process and, assuming that you had a positive experience, express your interest in future giveaways.

An important consideration: Because people who opted-in for the giveaway are likely to be inundated with emails from the event contributors, their email open rates and overall engagement will probably be lower than average, especially after they've gotten their gift. That's why, if you're contributing to a giveaway, your focus must be on delivering a top-quality resource and welcome email, which will tend to have the highest open rate.

4. Summits

Virtual summits seem to be popping up everywhere you look, especially in the coaching industry, and they continue to be effective ways to build your list and bring in revenue.

Virtual summits are the online version of a multi-speaker conference. You'll gather a group of experts to share their insights on the topic of the summit, and build an audience by offering free access to the presentations for a limited time.

After a period that varies between five and 21 days, free access to the presentations ends. The attendees have the option to purchase unlimited access to the summit recordings and bonuses. Those who decide to purchase the recordings can opt for an upsell (additional course or program that delves into the topic in greater depth).

If you decide to host your own summit to connect with influencers and grow your list, I suggest designing it with at least one upsell, so you can also build revenue.

Virtual summits are like giveaways because of the single opt-in page used to sign up for free access to the interviews or sessions. They're also similar to launches, because of the limited availability of the free content and discounted pricing. Usually, the introductory price for an "all-access pass" in a summit is half of the regular online price.

Just as with giveaways, you can either host a summit or participate as one of the speakers. You'll get the biggest impact to your list, revenue, and network of connections when you're the host, but that doesn't mean that you shouldn't consider participating as a speaker. I've built my list significantly and gained new clients as a result of the various summits I've been featured in.

When you're the host of the summit

Since summits tend to draw a larger number of subscribers than giveaways, and also because summits are a way to build instant authority, many coaches and trainers will be thrilled to participate in your summit.

You'll leverage your summit to connect with influencers, but that's not all! By hosting giveaways and summits, you become the influencer. You're the leader driving the audience to the event. The roles have switched!

Virtual summits require a great deal of preparation and a solid tech platform. You should seek expert help or at least support from technical virtual assistants to make the event successful.

If you decide to host a summit, apply the same relationship-building strategies that we explored for launches and giveaways:

- Create high-quality content by gathering a top team of expert speakers and providing actionable steps for your audience

- Host the summit on a reliable, easy-to-navigate tech platform

- Maintain clear lines of communication with the speakers

- Hold a debrief session after the event

- Continue building your relationship with the speakers

Also, don't expect your speakers to do all the promotion for your event. The responsibility to attract people to the summit lies in your hands, and the speakers' support should be considered a gift. If your promo requirements are too strict, you'll have a hard time getting a yes from top influencers.

When you want to be a guest speaker on a summit

When you're featured on a summit, you'll also be able to build your list, bring in revenue through affiliate commissions, and connect with influencers (the host and other speakers). Summits are like podcast interviews to the nth power, with n being the number of speakers in the summit!

As with giveaways, if you know that your connections lead summits on a regular basis or that they plan to host one, let them know at least six months in advance that you're interested in being a speaker. Always stress the value that you'd contribute to the event.

In many cases, summit hosts will have a minimum list-size and promo requirements for speakers. Because the hosts want to grow their list of subscribers and revenue, they seek the strongest partners for their venture.

In my experience, however, summit hosts who prioritize strict list-size and promo requirements are often not the best partners, because they evidently care only about their own gain from the event.

Always go with your gut feeling. If it doesn't feel like a win-win, step away.

Can you speak in a summit if you have a small list? Yes! If you've built a solid relationship with the host, he or she might agree to include you as a featured expert even if you don't meet the general requirements. Once again, delivering value first with the intention to create long-term relationships will pay off big-time.

If you're selected as a guest speaker, make sure you thoroughly prepare for your presentation with examples, case studies, and actionable items for the summit attendees.

Guest experts are usually expected to contribute a free gift for the event, so craft your free offer so that it helps you bring in the maximum number of new subscribers (part of your influencer marketing foundation).

Do as much as you can to promote the summit, including advertising. Prove that you're an advocate of the event, strengthening your relationship with the host and paving the way for future opportunities.

After the event, express your appreciation to your connection by mailing a thank-you note, creating a thank-you video, or simply by emailing. Also, share your insights about the process in a constructive way: What did you enjoy the most? What created the most value? What would you do differently?

Also, connect with the other speakers in the summit—a fast way to build your network. Before the event is over, when it's still top of mind, I usually send out LinkedIn and Facebook invitations to all speakers. Then, I ask some of them to be on my podcast so I can start supporting them right away.

Personal Story: Leveraging Joint Venture Partnerships as an Author by Karen Dimmick

"I've connected to a number of the leaders in my field in a couple of ways. One was via The Book Marketing Summit where I asked experts to speak on various topics around marketing a book. This positioned me in the industry as the book marketing expert, which was a huge benefit to the business. Since I coach entrepreneurs on writing a book that actively grows their business, I wanted to get similar influencer connections.

So, the way I'm currently focused on doing it, is to work out who in my industry provides complementary services to my business. Then I'm recommending their books from within my new books. I'm also asking one influencer to do a foreword for my book too, so when people search for their name in Amazon, my book will appear in the search results, while they get exposed to my audience.

For example, my latest book is on websites for authors, including the backend products and services, like courses and memberships. While email marketing is a natural extension of having a website, it's not my area of exper-tise. So, instead of trying to explain it in my book, I found people who teach email marketing specifically to authors. I told the reader it was out of the scope of the book and suggested they read these other books to get the information on how to do it.

When the book launches, I then ask them all to promote the book to their audience and that way we all get exposure to each other's audiences. It's a win-win-win. We each increase our reach and the readers get to hear about other experts that I trust and value, while getting the right information from people who really know their subject.

I started doing this back in 2014 with my second book and it really helped spread the word about the book and position me as an expert in the field. It's definitely a tactic I'll be doing for a long time and one I teach the entrepreneurs I coach as well.

A quick way to get started with it is to combine the two tactics I mentioned above and write an interview book. This is a book where you interview the influencers in your field, then add your own thoughts about what you learned from interviewing them. It's how I did my second book and was a great way to quickly get yourself known in a field and have your name mentioned alongside the top influencers in your niche. It can also be a great way to create a book if the writing process seems too overwhelming."

Karen Dimmick is a bestselling author, ghost writer, and host of The Book Marketing Summit. She helps entrepreneurs with a message write, publish, and market a book that grows their business. You can learn more about her at www.Bookthority.com

5. Intros

A simple yet powerful way to tap into your connections with coaches and trainers (and any category of influencer, for that matter) is to introduce them to new potential partners or potential clients.

To make it easier for them, create a customized short blurb for each kind of intro. For example, if the intro is for potential partners, you'd emphasize your experience, type of audience, and what you do to help that audience. If it's for potential clients, you'd put all your emphasis on the results you get for your clients.

It's important to be very clear about the kind of people you're interested in meeting. "I'm launching a book next year," you might say, "So I'd love to meet podcast hosts who could have me on their show."

About client referrals...

Things get a bit tricky when it comes to intros to potential clients. Since this is a direct referral, your connections must trust you and your ability to deliver results before they're ready to take that step. After all, their reputation is on the line. Ask for this kind of intro only when your relationship is mature and your connection is keenly aware of your offer's quality.

Many influencers have a formal referral system. Asking them if they have such a system is a good way to start the conversation. Also, consider offering a referral kit, which will make it simpler and less awkward for everyone involved.

What is a referral kit, and why is it so helpful?

Rather than sending prospects to a sales conversation with you (something many people are reluctant to do), your connections give them a resource (book, PDF, whitepaper, etc.) that you produce for potential clients. Within that resource, there will be an invitation to reach out to you so you can help them achieve the results they desire.

A lot less awkward, right?

In fact, your business partners will be eager to share your referral kit because they'll be giving something valuable to their own connections. You'll be helping them build goodwill within their own network!

After I created my referral kit, which includes my influencer marketing guide, my client referrals tripled.

Finally, offer a financial incentive for client referrals. Although money won't be the primary motivator for your connections to refer people to you, rewarding your connections for their support will help you earn their continued support.

Personal Story: The Power of an Introduction to the Right Person by Dave M. Lukas

"It is funny how things happen in life. If most people are honest, especially entrepreneurs, they have an idea of where they want to go, but don't really know how they are going to get there. You can plan for what you think is everything in your success journey, but once you start taking action, most of those plans get thrown out of the window. And that is because the road to success is not a straight line. It is a crazy, jumbled mess of things that don't ever seem to relate or coincide with each other as you are going through them—until one day, you look back and it becomes clear that all of the things you did seemed to follow a path and each one helped to get you where you are.

One thing I have noticed that is constant on life's journey is the power of the connections you make and the relationships you develop over the years.

I recently met James Altucher and got to spend some time with him. We connected and are now collaborating on some things together, but there is no way I could have ever imagined how I would meet James. Let me tell you the story.

Over a decade ago, I was introduced to a rising star in the Internet marketing and influencer world, Mike Koenigs. Mike is the king of video marketing online. He was hacking the Internet with video back in the '90s and to this day is still the go-to Internet marketing consultant to everyone from Tony Robbins to movie stars.

I met Mike in the early 2000s and honestly didn't really have a plan. I just knew he was someone I should meet. We hit it off, but never really did much together. We stayed in touch from time to time, but reconnected in the last few years and starting working together.

Mike invited me to a private event he was having for the 'who's who' of social media marketing. Attendees included Guy Kawasaki, John Lee Dumas, JJ Virgin, and a host of others. It was fun to attend and see a lot of people I had met over the years and make some new connections. One of those people was an amazing guy named Steve Olsher.

Steve and I connected on some common ideas and he asked me to speak at a conference he was hosting for people looking to pitch the top podcasters and 'icons' of the space. It was a blast. I met so many incredible people and made connections with a lot of the top podcasters whose shows I follow, and was surprised to find many of them followed mine.

At the event, Jeremy Ryan Slate of the Create Your Own Life podcast mentioned he was doing a live interview with James Altucher in New York City in the upcoming month. I checked, and just happened to be in the city that day.

Jeremy gave me a ticket and a month later, I was sitting front row at the private event.

Afterward, Jeremy introduced me to James and the story goes from there.

Think about that for a second: A chance meeting with Mike Koenigs over a decade ago led to me collaborating with James Altucher.

It is pretty amazing what the power of a connection and a relationship can accomplish. You just have to be open and willing to act on the opportunities when they present themselves.

I thank Mike because he has always been willing to help not just me, but anyone—whether it impacts him or not. That is a lesson I learned from him and practice in my life."

Dave M. Lukas is a serial entrepreneur, bestselling author, investor, and founder of the Misfit Entrepreneur Podcast. His companies have been on the Inc. 5000 list multiple times. He has been featured on radio, TV, and many top trade publications and websites such as Forbes, Inc., Yahoo! Finance, BTN, BTE, and others. He is the author of the Amazon bestseller The Ten-Year Career, The Fast Track to Retiring Young, Wealthy, and Fulfilled. The book is a culmination of five years of dedicated research into the mindset and habits of high performers, and gives the reader the missing links and a path to greater success and fulfillment. Learn more about Dave at www. MisfitEntrepreneur.com.

❧

The coaches and trainers in my network have played an important role in the growth of my business. If you decide to connect with coaches and trainers, follow the three steps below.

Take action!

Step 1: Write down your mission statement: "I will be introduced to the audience of_____ as (an interviewee, guest speaker, joint venture partner)."

Step 2: Put a target date on your calendar for beginning a collaboration with the coach or trainer.

Step 3: Apply what you learned in this chapter so you can achieve your goal! Don't aim for perfection. Just get going!

Chapter 11

Local Business Owners

....

Influencer marketing principle #11: If you do business with someone, they'll want to do business with you.

....

Is the owner of your popular local gym an influencer? Let's see...

Does she have a captive group of customers who work out at her facility? Yes!

Do her customers have the common goal of being healthier and fitter? Yes!

The gym owner is an influencer.

Local business owners are often not seen as influencers. But they have influence because of their captive audience of local clients who know and trust them.

Also, most local businesses have highly engaged email lists.

Think about it: When you get an email from your hair salon or your favorite ice cream shop, you're likely to open it. That's why connecting with local business owners opens the door to larger audiences than you might have expected.

Four-Step Process for Selecting Business Owner Connections

You should connect with business owners whose clientele matches your avatar, and whose business practices and products are aligned with your values and style. After all, your reputation will be linked to that of your local business partners.

To select the right business owners to connect with, follow a simple four-step process:

1. Make a list of all local businesses that might be a good fit. Base your first assessment on the audience those businesses serve, and how well it matches your ideal clients or customers.

For example, if you're a health coach, you'd create a list of yoga studios, day spas, meditation centers, hypnosis centers, chiropractic offices, and fitness centers.

2. Narrow down the list based on the products and services the businesses offer. Going back to the example of the health coach, if a yoga studio features health coaching services already, it might not be the best connection for you because you're a direct competitor.

3. Research the reputation of the business. Has it received mostly positive feedback? Great sources of information are Yelp. com, TripAdvisor.com (depending on the kind of business), reviews posted on their business Facebook page, and local Facebook groups.

Facebook groups are excellent sources of information. My town has a thriving Facebook group where residents ask for advice on the best doctors, plumbers, lawyers, etc., and group members aren't shy about sharing who they would and wouldn't recommend. You might want to join a similar group in your town and ask the members about their experiences with the business you have in mind.

4. Visit the business and become a customer. That's the best way to find out if the business matches your values and style, and whether you'd like to be associated with its brand.

Early in my business, when I wanted to share my message of personal empowerment, I researched local day spas in my town. I thought I could host a stress-management workshop. Although it had no reviews online, one of the spas seemed to be a great fit for my message. I was wrong! The poor customer service and lack of cleanliness in the facility helped me realize it wasn't a good match after all.

Take the time to do the research; it'll save you time and aggravation.

How to Connect with Local Business Owners

One of my clients is a private Spanish instructor. She often attracts new students through Meetups. For a nominal fee, she gathers groups of mid-level to advanced Spanish students for an informal conversation class. She develops a close connection with the participants, so when she offers her private services to them, they're usually eager to sign up.

When she decided to start her first group, she needed to find a suitable location for eight to 12 people. She thought of the local coffee shop, where there's a large space in the back that would be ideal for her Meetups.

My client is one of those people who cannot function in the morning without her cup o' joe, so she'd been a loyal customer of the coffee shop for years. "All I do is walk in the store and they rush to get my usual order," she said.

So, it was easy for her to get a yes when she asked the coffee shop owner for permission to host her Meetups in the back of the store. She was even granted a special place on the shop's bulletin board to promote her Meetup group.

The owner appreciates the additional business, and my client has a cozy and inviting place to bond with her potential clients. A clear win-win.

As you can see, the best way to connect with a local business owner is by becoming a loyal customer.

You don't need to be a customer for years before you can collaborate with your connection, but you do need to show from day one that you're a true advocate of their business.

To start, post a review of the business on Yelp.com, its Facebook business page, or the appropriate review site. Let the business manager or owner know that you've posted the review next time you see him or her.

Also, join the businesses' mailing lists. Pay close attention to:

- How often they communicate with their subscribers
- The kind of content they send out
- Any partner offers they might promote

This will give you an idea of the business owners' personality and style, so you can decide whether they are a good match or not.

By reading the emails they send to their customers, you'll learn more about the way they run their business. Also, you'll spot chances to deliver value. Constructive feedback and suggestions are usually welcome.

Pay attention to any special events the businesses offer. If they're used to creating partnerships, they'll be more open to collaborate.

In every interaction you have with the owner or manager, look for a chance to support the business. Remember that your #1 goal is to find ways to deliver value first.

Once you've become familiar with the business and have found at least one way to support it, then you'll be in a good position to start a relationship with the owner.

How to Set Yourself Up for Success When Partnering with Local Business Owners

Regardless of the idea you propose to the local business owner, pitch it from the position of how that idea will help them attract new customers and clients.

Compare the two scenarios below, as a health coach proposes her idea to Julie, the owner of a yoga studio:

First scenario: Hello, Julie. I'd like to give a presentation at your yoga studio on the best way to manage stress. I think your clients are a perfect fit for my stress-management program. What do you think?

Second scenario: Hello, Julie. I was thinking that people who are stressed could benefit so much from joining your yoga classes! Here's an idea: I could give a stress-management presentation right here at the studio. I'm sure it would attract new clients, plus your current clients would appreciate the message, too. What do you think?

Which scenario would be more appealing to Julie?

The way you position your pitch will determine whether you succeed or fail.

What's the best way to make your proposal?

You could pitch in person first, and then ask if the owner would like to see more details in writing. Alternatively, you could hand out a copy of your proposal on the spot and later email a copy.

Your approach will depend on your suggested project. A two-hour presentation, for example, will require a detailed proposal on the topic, logistics, and possible dates. A request to become referral partners can be handled through a face-to-face conversation.

Start with a small commitment. Once you've received the first yes, you'll be in a great position to continue growing the relationship and making the most of the connection.

How to Leverage Your Connections with Local Business Owners over the Long Term

Because of the wide variety of local businesses, it's not possible to cover all possible strategies within this book. You'll have to get creative to find suitable ways to collaborate with your target business owners.

If you create a solid connection, you might even be able to brainstorm ideas with the business owners on how to work together, which will increase their commitment to making those ideas a reality.

To get started, let's explore a couple of ways to collaborate with local business owners.

Local businesses as venues to share your message

You already know about the power of face-to-face speaking engagements and presentations in helping you gain new clients, but local libraries and associations are not the only places to give a presentation. Restaurants, yoga studios, and even practitioners' offices can be excellent venues for meeting potential clients.

Corrin, a friend who is a Certified Money Coach and Women's

Wealth Advisor, wanted to host a lunch-and-learn series as a way of building a sense of community and attracting potential clients.

As a regular customer of a local restaurant, it was easy for her to get a yes when she asked the owner if she could host her events there.

The restaurant owner benefits from the additional business brought by the luncheon attendees, and Corrin gets to position herself as an authority in her field and connect with her ideal clients.

Corrin has taken her initiatives to the next level, and invites guests to speak during her monthly events. As she deepens her connection with the speakers, they become a source of referrals for her business.

Also, if your expertise meets a need of the current business clientele, the business itself could promote you as a guest speaker. Just a few of the benefits:

- You connect with new potential clients among their captive audience.

- They deliver value to their current customers and clients.

- They attract new customers and clients by featuring your presentation.

The possibilities are endless…

- A parenting coach's presentation on the best toys for children's development would be ideal for a toy store.

- A health coach's training on a gluten-free lifestyle would be the perfect fit for a health food store.

- A party planner would be welcomed to provide party-planning tips at the cupcake store.

Everybody wins!

Are the ideas already percolating in your mind? I hope so!

Affiliate, joint venture, and referral partnerships

Like all other influencers, local businesses are seeking to complement their current offers.

If you're a meditation expert, you could partner with a local yoga studio as the preferred meditation teacher, or you could even host meditation sessions at the studio with a share of the revenue.

If you're a nutritionist, you could partner with local gyms for client referrals.

Remember that the partnership must have a clear and effective strategy. Avoid situations like the ones below:

- The owner tells you, "Sure, if I ever hear of an ideal client for you, I'll let you know!"

- The owner agrees to place your business cards on a side table (where no one will ever see them)

Have a candid conversation with the business owner about what each of you wants to get out of your relationship, including revenue share.

Once you've come to an agreement, staying in touch is essential. Your focus should remain on delivering value first, and continuously nurturing your relationship.

∽

Personal Story: Leveraging Connections with Local Influencers to Create a Competitive Advantage by Phoebe Chongchua

"Long before the days of this intricate online network that allows every company to be the media, there was only The

Media—radio, print, and TV news networks that determined the news of the day. That was a small group that controlled what the public saw, heard, and read. I was part of it—a TV journalist.

Today, for those of us who are content marketers, brand journalists (like I am now), or entrepreneurs, it's far easier to make our voices heard. We can socialize in online communities and reach consumers directly without needing to hound traditional news agencies to try to get our message to our core audience.

Then it might seem that digital marketing is entirely the way to go.

Not necessarily so. There are important lessons we can learn from the days before online marketing became the powerhouse it is. These strategies will improve your overall marketing reach and build stronger relationships with your audience.

In 1999 after the Columbine massacre, the ABC TV network I was working for in San Diego, California launched an initiative to curtail violence by helping at-risk boys. Specifically, we wanted to recruit 1,000 male mentors for these young boys. But how?

I knew there had to be two things:

- *Something that attracted the public to want to participate—a place where they wanted to go and learn how they could help.*

- *A group of core influencers or Champions (as I called them).*

The result? I created a one-day Resource Festival that in just four years attracted 20,000 people.

The event was no easy task to host. It required collaborative efforts, great community influencers, strong storytellers, and significant reach.

We formed a core team of 20 Champions (influencers) from businesses and non-profit organizations. This group met and brainstormed and would end up doing a large part of the word-of-mouth work to make the day successful. The event, which was at first only booths in year one, grew into an interactive festival that offered resources for the entire community from the young to the elderly.

There were four stages with daylong entertainment. There were educational seminars on home buying. There was an identity-theft protection zone with a chance to get your documents shredded for free, a car seat safety check, a job fair that hired 330+ people in one day, prizes, music, food, and, fun! The Padres, the Chargers, and the station's TV news anchors signed autographs. The county declared it "10Leadership Day!" It was the place to be for the help you needed.

What made it work?

Three key ingredients:

1. *The public's interest drove the creation of the event. We understood our audience's needs.*

2. *Emotional and informational storytelling about topics the news media was ignoring.*

3. *Most importantly, our team of Champions (influencers) helped us share and spread a unified message.*

An event like this takes the right influencers, the best

stories, and a passion to help your core audience. This strategy builds lifelong fans. Couple it with your PR efforts and digital content marketing such as a successful blog or podcast, and you have a competitive advantage that catapults your business to dominate your marketplace."

Phoebe Chongchua is a multimedia brand journalist, consultant, and marketing strategist who makes brands remarkable. Using her skills as a TV news journalist, she connects brands and consumers through powerful storytelling. Companies gain a competitive advantage when they learn to "Be the Media." Phoebe is a "Top 50 Podcaster to Follow." Learn more about Phoebe at TheBrandJournalismAdvantage.com and listen to The Brand Journalism Advantage podcast at www.ThinkLikeAJournalist.com.

Remember, opportunities to grow your business through partnerships with local business owners are all around you.

You can start by thinking of how you could work with the businesses you currently support as a customer. Also, you could just drive around town and look for opportunities you haven't noticed yet.

Committed to partnering with local business owners? Then follow the three steps below.

Take Action!

Step 1: Write down your mission statement: "I will be introduced to the audience of_____ as (a guest speaker, joint venture partner, other form of collaboration)."

Step 2: Put a target date on your calendar for beginning a collaboration with the business owner.

Step 3: Apply what you learned in this chapter so you can achieve your goal! Don't aim for perfection. Just get going!

Chapter 12

What about Celebrities and Well-Known Experts? Special Considerations

....

Influencer marketing principle #12: Building connections with celebrities and well-known experts may have a place in your influencer outreach efforts, but should never take over your entire campaign.

....

Top athletes, Hollywood stars, bestselling authors, well-known speakers, elite fashion designers, renowned artists, and other well-known experts can be considered celebrities.

Thanks to the power of new media channels such as YouTube, and social media, there has been an influx of new online celebrities, such as makeup demonstrator Michelle Phan, whose YouTube channel has millions of followers and over a billion views.

As a result, there might be a wide range of celebrities who could potentially help you exponentially grow your business if you gained their endorsement.

If you have the chance to benefit from the Oprah effect or the like, of course, you should go for it!

Your first step should always be to learn as much as you can about the celebrity in question, and become a true supporter and advocate of their message. The principles you learned in the chapter dedicated to the mindset to connect with influencers (Chapter 3) apply to celebrities, too.

However, because of the volume of inquiries celebrities receive, you must be prepared to spend considerable time and effort to earn their attention and get past the gatekeepers.

As always, adding a personalized touch to your attempts to connect with the influencer will go a long way. One of my podcast guests, a world-renowned speaker and bestselling author, said that his gatekeepers screen his emails, and only forward messages with a carefully crafted personal story.

Ask yourself how the celebrity has impacted your life, and express your feelings candidly in writing, audio, or video. Don't attempt to gain a celebrity's endorsement in your first communication. Remember: Delivering consistent value always comes first.

Other celebrities I interviewed on my podcast revealed that the only way to connect with them is through mutual introductions. As your network expands, you might meet someone who knows the celebrity you intend to meet.

When you ask for the introduction, be sure that your relationship has reached the maturity stage, and that the person knows the celebrity well enough.

For example, I wouldn't be able to introduce people to some of the celebrities I've had on my show because the extent of my relationship with those celebrities was limited to the interview.

When connecting with celebrities, you need to anticipate more extensive follow-up, and your efforts won't pan out in many cases.

That's why I suggest that your influencer outreach mix include:

- A significant number of niche influencers who will be easier to connect with and will probably help you move your business forward much sooner

- A few celebrities and well-known experts if you so desire

I encourage you to ask yourself why it's so important for you to connect with a certain celebrity or expert. It's easy to idolize someone, and see that person as the only one who can help you when, in reality, there are many people who are more accessible and could have an even larger impact on your business.

One way to take advantage of the influence of celebrities without having to reach them directly is to appear as a guest on a show or at an event where they have also appeared, such as network TV shows, high-profile podcasts, or major conferences. Focus on creating connections that will lead you to be featured in such venues and, as a result, "borrow authority" from the celebrity guests. Such appearances can be game changers for your personal brand and your business.

In the end, the philosophy to connect with celebrities and well-known experts is the same as that to connect with niche influencers. It all starts with the desire to deliver value and your belief that it's possible to create the connection.

Take action!

Step 1: Name five celebrities you'd like to connect with.

Step 2: Visualize yourself creating a business relationship with each person on your list. Does it feel possible?

Step 3: Focus on celebrity connections that feel possible and exciting for you.

PART 3

FINE-TUNING YOUR INFLUENCER MARKETING STRATEGY

Chapter 13

Your Influencer Marketing System

Influencer marketing principle #13: Trust the process—and don't skip steps—when connecting with influencers.

S o far, you've learned **how to overcome common obstacles** that might have prevented you from connecting with influencers in the past.

You **discovered the mindset to connect with influencers** and **the foundation** for a successful influencer marketing campaign.

Then, you explored the **tactics to select influencers** so you know whether a particular influencer is right for you or not.

You learned **the main six influencer categories**: how to select the influencers within the category, how to connect with them, how to set yourself up for success, and how to leverage your connection over the long term.

In a few words, you've learned **the framework for success with influencer marketing that leads to long-term connections and sustainable business growth**.

In this section, you'll find:

- A summary of the influencer marketing blueprint and a deeper exploration of the relationship-building stages
- How to manage your time effectively as you create and nurture your network

The Blueprint of a Successful Influencer Marketing Strategy

The blueprint of a successful influencer marketing strategy includes seven components:

1. Building your foundation
2. Selecting your connections: your top 50
3. Pinpointing your main objective per influencer
4. Initiating the connections
5. Nurturing your connections
6. Tracking your connections
7. Making the most of your influencer outreach efforts

Building Your Foundation

You've learned what it takes to be "influencer ready." This doesn't mean that once you're ready, you'll be ready forever. Your foundation is dynamic, and it will evolve with your business.

Since I became an entrepreneur in 2003, my avatar, products, programs, and even my core mission have changed multiple times. I've gone from helping high school and college students move to the next level in their education to assisting job seekers with their search efforts, to working side-by-side with entrepreneurs as they grow their business. The right influencers for me have also changed. I'm certain that more changes are on the way.

Has your business changed since the beginning of your journey? If you're nodding your head, now you know you're not alone!

I encourage you to do a quarterly review of your strategy and business efforts.

Make changes to your foundation depending on the strategic direction you want for your business.

Selecting Your Connections: Your Top 50

We've talked about how to select the right influencers. But what happens afterward? One of the best tools I use to succeed with influencer marketing is my "top 50" list. That list includes my closest connections.

I encourage you to create a top-50 list. You'll use the list as a constant reminder to build and nurture your most important connections.

Why 50 people and not 100? I chose 50 because that number is manageable for me. If you feel you can effectively manage 100 close business relationships, go for it.

What matters is that you feel capable of fully supporting them and dedicating enough time to the relationships so that your efforts lead to positive tangible outcomes.

Just like your foundation, your top-50 list will be dynamic. From time to time, I cross out names on the list and add new names as my relationships and business evolve.

What information should you include on your top-50 list? Below is the information I have on my list, which I keep in a simple Excel sheet:

- Name

- Website
- Contact info (email, physical mailing address, phone number)
- How you met
- What matters most to him or her (intros, social media exposure, JV partnerships, etc.)
- Possible ways to tap into the connection

The last item helps me keep my main objective top of mind. Let's explore that in a bit more detail.

Pinpointing your main objective per influencer connection

You've learned you can benefit from influencer connections in myriad ways, such as:

- Guest appearances that build authority and grow your list of subscribers
- Referrals
- Introductions to other influencers
- Introductions to potential partners and affiliates
- Business partnerships
- Learning and inspiration

Keeping in mind that your primary objective during the relationship should always be to deliver as much value as possible, you also need to define how you would ideally want to leverage your connections.

With a clear goal in mind, you'll be able to focus your actions and get results much faster.

If your primary goal is to grow your list, for example, you'll focus on guest appearances. If you're going to launch a new program, your focus will be on creating new business partnerships.

Often, as your relationships mature, you'll collaborate with your connections in multiple ways.

For example, one of my closest connections first had me as a guest on his podcast (the reason I initially approached him), but then he introduced me to a large number of influencers, including podcast and summit hosts. We've also helped each other with client referrals. He has become a good friend now, and I continue doing whatever I can to support him and his business.

Initiating the connections

Your next step is to start relationships with your ideal influencers. Earlier in this book, you learned the main influencer categories and how to reach out to people within each category.

There's only one more consideration: creating rapport.

Many of my closest connections started because I had something in common with them: a value or belief, a challenge, or a simple preference.

Isn't that how most relationships start? You join a hiking group and become friends with your fellow hikers, or you bond with someone waiting in line at the grocery store because both of you bought the same brand of Greek yogurt.

You've heard about the nervous job applicant who eyes a sports-themed mug at the hiring manager's office, and how he ups his chance of landing the job when he says, "I'm a fan, too!"

When you establish rapport early on, it's easier for you to develop that relationship.

Do you share a favorite sports team?

Are you both passionate about a specific topic?

Do you have a similar upbringing?

Have you gone through similar struggles?

Did you both grow up in the same town?

Those are just a few ways to establish rapport early in the relationship.

Nurturing your connections

Initiating the connection is only the first step on the road to building a strong relationship with the influencer. What comes next is continued support (nurturing the connection).

Nurturing your connections means providing value continuously, not just at the beginning of the relationship and when you need their help—an easy way to destroy goodwill.

In the mindset section of this book, you learned different ways to support your influencer connections. At least once a month, act on those ideas or come up with your own way to support your top 50 connections.

That's what I do in my business. You don't have to spend hours per connection. Small gestures that count are:

- Sharing one of their social media posts
- Writing an insightful comment on their blog post
- Checking in to see how their recent launch went
- Replying to their newsletter if something they wrote resonated with you
- Sharing a software tool or shortcut you've recently discovered

I might miss a month if my schedule is especially hectic, but overall, my connections know I'm there for them. I encourage you to do the same.

Tracking your connections

It's easy to let the day-to-day grind get in the way of relationship building. The best way to prevent that is by having a system to track your influencer marketing efforts.

You could do something as simple as maintaining a spreadsheet. In one tab, you can track your interactions with existing business relationships, and in another tab, your progress on initiating new influencer connections.

"That sounds like a lot of work," you might be thinking. Yes, building a solid network of influencer connections takes time and dedication, especially early in the game.

As your circle of connections grows and strengthens, it'll become second-nature and much less time-consuming to keep your influencer relationships healthy.

The importance of following up

When you want to connect with influencers, following up is a must. Influencers are busy people who tend to be swamped with connection requests. Those who follow up will stand out from the crowd.

I often hear from people who feel frustrated that influencers don't get back to them. "It's too difficult to reach out to influencers," they say. Or "It's impossible to get past the gatekeepers." When I ask, "Did you follow up?" the answer is usually no.

I've had to follow up three times (or more) to get an answer. If I pitch my idea to a podcast and they tell me they'll start recording again in two months, I follow up then. If, after the two months, they say they need two more months, I follow up again. In most cases, my pitch is accepted. Persistence wins!

To track when you need to follow up and with whom, you may add a simple note in Google Calendar. You can also use automated tools like Followupthen.com and Boomerangapp.com.

How many times should you follow up?

The answer depends on the influencer, but as a rule of thumb, I suggest you follow up three times.

However, you need to be strategic about what you say in your second or third attempt. It's insane to expect different results when you don't change your approach.

Once, when I was having a hard time reaching one of my connections, I decided to send a message to one of his team members, who asked him to check his spam folder. Problem solved! At the time, what I planned to do next if Plan B didn't work was to send him a tweet. And if that didn't work, I was going to use LinkedIn. You'll have to be creative if you want to succeed with your follow-ups!

Also, it's important to wait a few days between messages or calls. I tend to wait a week, which gives the other person plenty of time to process my request without feeling that I'm pestering him or her.

If you've supported the influencers in the ways we've discussed, they'll be very responsive, so it's likely that you won't have to follow up too many times—unless your messages are stuck in a spam folder!

When to give up

A question I'm asked often is, "When should I give up?" The answer also depends on the influencer and what you've done to support them.

For example, let's say you've been trying to connect with a podcaster.

You've supported the podcast on social media by sharing their posts and adding insightful comments.

You've written a 5-star review of the show on iTunes.

You've pitched your idea for an interview three times.

But all you've gotten so far is… crickets.

If that's the case, then it might be time to give up.

What if you're not ready to give up yet? Then, wait a few weeks to follow up again (this time with a different pitch or idea). In the meantime, continue supporting him or her in any way you can.

Intuitively, you'll know when it's time to let go. Trust your intuition, and remember that there are many other influencers who might be more receptive to you, and who might become more valuable connections in the future than the unresponsive people.

Making the most of your influencer outreach efforts

When we explored the main six influencer categories, you learned how to make the most of your influencer outreach.

Here, I'd like to explore general strategies (applicable to all categories) that will make the outreach process as successful as possible.

When to ask for support

I'm often asked *when* it's appropriate to ask for a guest appearance, intro, referral, joint promo, etc. No matter whom you intend to ask, the right time to ask for support depends on the magnitude of your request.

Let's say you move into a new neighborhood and have recently met the neighbors. You'd probably think it's acceptable to ask to borrow their hose, but do you think it would be appropriate to ask them to babysit your kids or to take care of your guinea pig while you're away?

The same idea applies to your relationships with influencers.

The rule of thumb is:

Small request = Early stage of the relationship

Big request = Mature stage of the relationship

The biggest requests are those that require more time, commitment, and trust from the influencer, such as joint venture partnerships and referrals.

Also, keep in mind that as you provide value and support to the influencer, the natural desire to reciprocate may make the process easier for you. They might jump ahead and offer to support you without your having to ask.

That said, in many (if not most) situations, you'll have to ask for what you want to get what you want. Never assume they can read your mind—they're focused on sharing their own message and growing their own business.

How to ask for support

You've learned how to connect and how to "get in" with the major categories of influencers. However, there are general principles that apply to all influencer outreach efforts, as you'll see below.

Use the medium they prefer

When I got my first corporate job, a mentor told me, "The first thing you want to ask is how people like to communicate. Some people love email and others hate it. Same with text and voice mail messages." He was right! Whenever I reached out to my colleagues using the medium they preferred, I got through to them fast! The same applies to your influencer connections.

For example, if you know that the person is on Facebook all the time, and uses Facebook chats for business communications, don't send an email or LinkedIn message.

I dislike Facebook chat for business, but many people try to reach me that way. I still reply to them and ask them to email me, but others who have the same preference might just ignore them because it's the "wrong" medium. So, do your research!

Position your request as a favor to them

What would appeal to you more?

1. Someone who mentions they saw you driving your daughter to soccer practice, and wants to know if you'd like to start a carpool so you don't have to drive her all the time.

2. Someone who asks you if you could give their kid a ride to soccer practice.

My point: Always emphasize how your request will benefit the other person's business and audience.

A request to interview you = *Valuable content for their audience*

A joint venture partnership = *Solution to fill unmet audience needs + Added revenue for their business*

Referrals = *Valuable resource for their contacts + Added revenue in the form of referral incentives*

Remember, influencers aren't different from any other human being: It's always about them—never about you.

Always follow up

I can't stress enough the importance of following up.

Be persistent and you'll get an answer. If that answer is a no, it's okay. At least you'll know you need to move on.

Managing your time effectively as you create and nurture your network

You learned in Chapter 2 of this book that a common misconception that prevents entrepreneurs from applying influencer marketing tactics is to assume that influencer marketing will take hours a day or that it takes years to gain the attention of influencers.

If that were the case, I wouldn't have written this book.

But how can you avoid such a dire scenario?

The answer lies in creating habits and focusing on what works.

What does that mean? That you'll be successful when:

1. You create a system in which you're habitually creating, nurturing, and collaborating with your network.

2. You've applied the strategies you've learned in this book, so that you:

   • Dedicate your time and effort only to connecting with those who are a perfect match.

   • Agree only to forms of collaboration that will move your business forward.

That's what I've done to build and leverage a strong network of influencers in only a couple of hours a week.

Assuming that you've already built your influencer marketing foundation, the influencer marketing system I use and recommend is based on the strategic components you just learned:

   • Selecting new influencers and pinpointing your main objective

   • Initiating new connections

- Nurturing existing relationships
- Tapping into your network

To create your system, you must follow four steps:

1. Break down the components of the system into tasks
2. Decide the resources needed for each task
3. Schedule tasks and enter them into a tracking tool
4. Take action and follow your schedule

Next, you'll learn the step-by-step process to implement the system in your business.

1) Break down the components of the system into tasks

Let's assume you've already built a solid influencer marketing foundation.

A sample list of influencer marketing tasks is as follows.

Selecting new influencers and pinpointing your main objective

1. Pick a tracking tool, such as a simple spreadsheet or paid software like pipedrive.com, to house the information about your connections
2. Research potential connections
3. Enter information in the tracking tool
4. Decide who to reach out to (only perfect matches qualify)

5. Decide main objective per connection and update tracking tool

Initiating new connections

1. Decide the best way to approach each person

2. Reach out to them using the most effective medium

3. Track communications

Nurturing existing relationships

1. Decide the top ways to deliver value

2. Add room in your schedule for support efforts

3. Take action weekly to deliver value to your existing connections

Tapping into your network

1. Pitch ideas that will move your business forward

2. Track the progress of your pitches

3. Track the results from each collaboration

4. Decide which efforts to continue and which to phase out

5. Follow up on proposals and next steps

2) Determine the resources needed for each task

I outsource administrative tasks such as research. That's how I can focus on what's most impactful for building and nurturing my network: relationship building.

Train your virtual assistant (VA) on exactly what information you need per influencer. Make it easy for him or her to succeed by providing tracking tools and a written description of the process to follow.

For example, I created a Google sheet for potential podcaster connections. My VA spends a couple of hours a week researching podcasts that might be a good fit, and I take a few minutes once a week to review the results of her research and decide who I want to reach out to.

3) Schedule tasks and enter them into a tracking tool

A simple tool like Google Calendar can help you keep track of your tasks. Timing apps assist you with managing your time.

An eye-opening exercise is to log every business task you complete per day for a week. At the end of the week, you'll see how many hours you *really* spend on each activity.

When I did that, my jaw dropped. I was spending over four hours a week on Facebook groups, something that wasn't making a big difference in my business. Now, I set a timer, and allow myself only 20 minutes a day for social media groups.

When you incorporate influencer marketing into your business, you'll also need to keep track of related tasks.

Ask yourself whether your daily business activities are:

1. Aligned with your mission and values

2. Helping you achieve your immediate business goals

3. Moving your business forward

Do more of what works and less of what doesn't. This is easier said than done, especially when you have a routine, and feel comfortable with the status quo. But if you want your business to grow, you've got to take the plunge and protect your time.

To batch or not to batch?

The decision to batch influencer marketing tasks depends on what you're trying to accomplish. If you're going to reach out to podcasters, for example, submitting several pitches at once rather than one at a time would be most effective.

I designate one day of the week to nurture my network. For example, every Friday, I get a Google Calendar reminder to check what's new with my closest business relationships and find opportunities to support them.

When I know someone has an upcoming launch, I enter the dates in my promotional calendar so I can provide as much support as possible.

I also spend time every week working toward collaboration with new and existing connections. That might include brainstorming sessions on how to best collaborate, reaching out to local organizations for potential speaking engagements, strategizing joint webinars, pitching ideas for podcast appearances, or writing a guest post.

4) Take action and follow your schedule

As you know, reminders are not enough to get positive results. Consistent action is a must.

Just like a trickle of water that carves a stone, each minute you spend building your network will have a long-lasting impact on your business… and life!

What it all comes down to...

The influencer marketing process should never feel like dreadful work. Instead, each new connection should bring an influx of positive energy and excitement to your business.

Avoid becoming too "scientific" and bogged down by feeling you have to fill out an "influencer marketing report" every week. Who wants that?

Instead, simplify.

Start by building one connection and nurture that connection. Then, build the next.

Make it your goal to deliver as much value as possible to those you meet, stay organized, follow through, and you'll see positive results.

Celebrate every time you meet someone you can relate to, or when you find new ways to collaborate with your connections. Reward yourself—you deserve it!

Building a solid foundation and staying on track when you implement this system is the core mission of my individual and group coaching programs.

I designed the programs with the mission to provide step-by-step guidance to help you achieve results much faster than if you'd tried to do it all on your own. I know that if you see positive results, then you'll want to "stick with the plan" and continue taking action.

Also, I provide support and accountability to stay on track, which can prove challenging when you implement a new strategy on your own. *You can find more information about the programs in the resources section at the end of this book.*

Take action!

Write down your mission statement: **"I will connect with _____ influencers in the next ___weeks, and I will build long-lasting relationships with them."**

Now, let's make this happen!

Chapter 14

What to Do When Influencer Marketing Goes Wrong

....

Influencer marketing principle #14: In influencer marketing, what matters is not whether things go wrong, but what you do when bad things happen.

....

In an ideal world, you connect with influencers who are perfectly in tune with your values and personality.

They take note of your support from day one and your relationships start to blossom.

When you're asked how you've created such good connections, you say, "We instantly clicked!"

After a while, they're eager to help you grow your business. They offer their support before you even ask.

Soon after, you find yourself sharing your message with new audiences made up of your ideal clients, who see you as an authority in your field.

Your list of subscribers skyrockets.

The balance in your bank account matches the growth of your list.

As you make a significant positive impact in the world, you feel that you're leaving a legacy for generations to come.

Imagine if that happened to you? How would you feel?

Even though you can achieve amazing results with influencer marketing, the process will probably deviate from the plan. Ideal scenarios aren't the norm.

Influencer marketing takes hard work and dedication, and yes, you'll face rejection and disappointment. That's why I want to dedicate this section to those unpleasant situations that you might encounter. This way, you'll know what to do when things go wrong.

I'm not a fan of focusing on negative scenarios, but being prepared for the worst will not only help you get ahead if things don't go according to plan, but will give you the peace of mind required to continue making progress with your influencer outreach.

The influencers are unresponsive

If you've taken the time to become an advocate of your influencer connections, it's very unlikely that they'll be unresponsive.

But it could happen…

Even when you follow up several times and in different ways, you might not hear back from them.

That's when you need to ask yourself how relevant and important those relationships are for the growth of your business.

Read the section in this book titled "When to Give Up" again. Once you make a decision, follow through. It's easy to be ambivalent and continue to follow up half-heartedly, which will be a waste of time.

The influencers change their mind

A "yes, let's collaborate" from an influencer feels fantastic, but like a handshake, it's not a binding contract—unless you make it so. Everyone's business needs are constantly changing, including those of influencers.

For formal business partnerships, you'll need legal support and a contract, but for more informal collaborations such as interviews, summits, joint webinars, guest posts, etc., you'll have to trust that the other person keeps his or her word.

Here's how to prepare in case your connections change their mind about supporting you.

Never put all your eggs in one basket. The growth of your business should never depend on one product, one marketing channel, or one business partner. If you find yourself in that situation, make it a priority to diversify your efforts and expand your network.

Clearly communicate your expectations. For example, if someone promises to promote your webinar to their audience, get agreement on firm dates for the promotion. Put in writing how many emails and social media posts the campaign requires and confirm that your proposal is acceptable to the other person. Negotiate until there's a clear agreement. The clearer you are up-front, the more you'll lessen the risk of the influencers backing out.

Make supporting you as easy as possible for the other person. An overwhelmed influencer is someone who cancels non-essential commitments (e.g. the commitment with you). Make sure you provide everything they might need to support you. For example, in a joint venture promotion, provide swipe files, images, links, a clear promo calendar, and continuous reminders that will save your partner time and effort.

Confirm well ahead of time. Always confirm an appearance or collaborative campaign well in advance. It's acceptable to confirm the day before a media appearance, but you should get confirmation for joint promotions and speaking engagements at least three to four weeks in advance.

The influencers don't keep their promises

This is an issue that often surfaces with joint venture launches.

In contrast to evergreen (year-round) offers, launches involve a small promotional window and a tight schedule that represents a big commitment for all partners involved.

Joint venture launches also require careful coordination and a fair amount of administrative work.

That's why your connection's plans to promote your launch might be the first thing to go when it's time to trim the schedule.

If they let you know ahead of time about their change in plans, you can prepare, and there's always room for future collaboration as you continue your relationships.

However, bad surprises happen…

A few not-so-great situations you could face are:

The lack-of-planning partners

They agree to work with you and promote your offers without having carefully looked at their promo schedule. Then, when they go back to their desks and check, they realize they can't fit you in, but they neglect to tell you.

Others agree to work with you but forget to set up the promotion (or to ask their staff to do so). They're so busy running their business that they decide at the last minute to cut out your promo. In the hustle and bustle of their day-to-day work, they never let you know of the change in plans.

When you check the launch stats, you realize your partner never promoted you.

The passive-resistant partners

Your partners agree to fully collaborate with you during your launch, but they support you half-heartedly.

Instead of following the promo schedule, mailing their subscribers as promised, and truly believing in what you have to offer, they send out a couple of tweets or post once on Facebook.

When you check your stats, you see they generated five clicks and no subscribers (or buyers).

The irresponsible partners

Sometimes the issue is rooted in personality and values. They simply might not feel they have to honor their promise, so they don't (and they never tell you).

Later, your stats reveal what happened. When you try to contact them, they never get back to you.

The just-changed-my-mind partners

Your partners change their mind about collaborating with you for various reasons that are valid for them (a gut feeling, last-minute commitment, another promotion that might suit their business better, etc.). The problem is that they never tell you of their new plan, so you're in for a nasty surprise when you check your launch stats.

What can you do to prevent the situations above?

If you and the other person haven't really gotten to know each other well or if your partner doesn't really know your business and your products, there's a high risk for these bad situations to happen. The problems are almost always rooted in a relationship that isn't deep enough.

That's why it's essential to take the time to build a well-nurtured, mature relationship if you want to succeed with joint venture partnerships and other complex forms of collaboration such as combined offers and joint webinars.

What can you do after the fact?

When I've been let down by a partner in the ways I've mentioned, even if I think we know each other very well, I let go of the relationship.

For me, it's not worth spending precious time and effort on that connection when I could be nurturing relationships with those who truly appreciate me and support me.

In the end, it's up to you to decide. But keep in mind that people's behaviors tend to repeat themselves—even negative behaviors.

The connections never reach the maturity stage

Sometimes you might initiate the connections. However, even though the influencers express gratitude for your support, they're routinely unresponsive when you attempt to take the relationship "to the next level" by asking to meet with them or to brainstorm collaboration ideas.

You might even land an interview on the influencer's show, but after the interview airs, the influencer becomes unresponsive.

This situation happens most commonly when the other person has a large audience and an inbox flooded with requests for collaboration. However, it could also happen with niche influencers.

You know we're all "busy," but we make time for what we feel will benefit us. That's why, regardless of the audience size of the influencer, that kind of behavior shows that the person doesn't see value in furthering a relationship with you.

If this happens, you could do two things:

Deepen the relationship by delivering even more value

Instead of asking for their help, just come up with new ways to support the influencers in question. Try to ask for support again when you feel that the time is right. If they're still unresponsive, you may decide to focus on other priorities instead.

Move on

If you feel that you've done everything you can to support the influencer and deliver value, it's okay to shift your attention to other connections with whom you'll be able to relate and collaborate.

Bottom line: Just like with personal relationships, you can't force a connection. In time, as you expand your network, it'll be clear to you who is and isn't a good candidate for a long-term connection.

The influencers' actions are misaligned with your goals or values

One of the guests on my "Beyond Influencer Marketing" podcast shared a story about how, after making a significant investment in a mastermind with high-profile entrepreneurs, he realized that his values and that of the leader of the group were mismatched.

When he invested in the mastermind, he thought the group was perfect for what he wanted to achieve. Looking back, he reflected on that tough lesson learned and stressed the importance of finding clear value alignment before taking the next step with a business relationship.

Something similar might happen to you. You might feel as though you've found the perfect influencer to connect with: Perfect audience. Perfect content. Everything's just right!

However, as you get to know the person, you might realize that you were wrong. People are on their best behavior when you first meet them, and time will tell whether they're truly a good match for you.

Also, people (and their business) change. And with change come messages and behaviors that might not be aligned with your mission, brand, goals, or values.

I once met a niche influencer who seemed to be a perfect match. He was eager to further the relationship, and soon we found ways to collaborate. However, a few months after we met, he stopped replying to my emails. It was such a huge change in behavior that I worried something terrible had happened to him.

However, three months later, he finally wrote to announce he now had a manager who'd be dealing with all his business partners. I set up a time to talk to the new manager, who told me about their "new policies." Those policies involved sales practices that were against my values and business mission, so I had to let go of that relationship.

In my mind, there's only one thing to do when there's a goal or value mismatch: move on.

Take action!

When things don't go according to plan, remember what Marianne Williamson once said: "I trust that when people meet, we meet for a transcendent reason, and that the challenges we face in life are always lessons that serve our soul's growth."[20]

Chapter 15

What's Next for You?

....

Influencer marketing principle #15: The value-first mindset should permeate through every thought and action in your influencer marketing efforts.

....

A s you've gone through the previous chapters in this book, you've learned 14 powerful influencer marketing principles:

....

Influencer marketing principle #1: Building a strong network of influencer connections can transform your business—and your life.

Influencer marketing principle #2: Only you decide if common roadblocks will stop you from connecting with influential people.

Influencer marketing principle #3: When you prepare to connect with influencers with the belief that you can succeed, you will succeed.

Influencer marketing principle #4: You'll get the most out of your influencer outreach when you build a solid foundation.

Influencer marketing principle #5: Not every influencer will be right for you—and that's okay.

Influencer marketing principle #6: Podcasters let you amplify your voice to extraordinary levels.

Influencer marketing principle #7: Bloggers help you transform your writing into a vehicle for building a long-lasting legacy.

Influencer marketing principle #8: People trust in your expertise when you share it on TV.

Influencer marketing principle #9: Your best influencer connections might be in your own backyard.

Influencer marketing principle #10: The fast-growing coaching and training industry expands your options to connect with influencers.

Influencer marketing principle #11: If you do business with someone, they'll want to do business with you.

Influencer marketing principle #12: Building connections with celebrities and well-known experts may have a place in your influencer outreach efforts, but should never take over your entire campaign.

Influencer marketing principle #13: Trust the process—and don't skip steps—when connecting with influencers.

Influencer marketing principle #14: In influencer marketing, what matters is not whether things go wrong, but what you do when bad things happen.

. . . .

However, there's one overarching principle you must keep in mind throughout your outreach efforts and as you nurture your connections, a principle that must always guide your actions:

Value comes first

Giving comes first

Serving comes first

It's only when you adopt the value-first mindset that you'll get value in return as a result of your influencer marketing efforts.

What's next?

You now know what it takes to build long-lasting connections with influential people to grow your business, but that's only the first step.

As Leonardo da Vinci once said, "Knowing is not enough; we must apply. Being willing is not enough; we must do."[21]

Act now

First, choose one small action you can take *right now* to apply the strategies you've learned in this book. Making a list of potential influencer connections is a great place to start.

If you feel tempted to wait till tomorrow, go back to the mindset section earlier in this book. Being "too busy" or this being "not the right time" might be a subconscious way of rationalizing a mindset block. Don't become your own obstacle to success.

Get help

Seek expert help as you build your influencer marketing foundation and apply the influencer marketing strategies you've learned. Early in my business, I tried to go it alone and figure things out on my own, and after making costly mistakes, I looked back with regret, wishing I had sought expert help from day one.

Having read *Beyond Influencer Marketing*, you have a great deal of information and practical steps to leverage influencer marketing in your business. However, there are key elements I'm unable to provide to you through this book alone:

- **A clear path to apply the influencer marketing principles *in your particular situation.*** For example, you might need to focus on strengthening your foundation first through a new opt-in funnel or referral kit. Based on your market, you might need to focus only on one category of influencer. If you're confused about what to do next, you'll probably do nothing and remain stuck. Trying things out to "see how it works" might leave you as burned out as before, wondering why you're not getting the results you expected. On the other hand, if you know from day one exactly what to do to succeed, you'll be empowered to take action and will see positive results quickly.

- **Accountability.** When life gets in the way you won't procrastinate. Instead, you will be inspired to stay focused and continue to make progress.

- **Expert guidance from someone who is invested in the success of your business.** Even though everything might seem very straightforward right now, you will have questions as you go along. Not having someone to steer you in the right direction will make you waste time and money. The danger of this situation is that you might eventually say to yourself, "Well, it didn't work for me," and never get to experience the amazing opportunities that were waiting for you just around the corner. Instead, if you have an expert guide who's there for you to answer all your questions, you will reach (and exceed) your goals much faster.

Let's explore how I can personally guide you, step by step, as you build a solid marketing foundation and a powerful network of influencer connections. Start by going to www.cloriskylie.com/consultation.

I have faith in you.

It's time for you to truly and fully *reveal your magnificence!*

Cloris

Acknowledgments

I'm deeply grateful for everyone who contributed to the creation of *Beyond Influencer Marketing.*

Thanks to the fantastic members of the *Beyond Influencer Marketing* launch team for your timely feedback and support.

Thanks to my editor, Robert Macias, and my awesome book production team for doing your finest work to make this a top-quality book.

Much gratitude to my amazing friends who contributed their personal stories to the book. In alphabetical order: Phoebe Chongchua, JV Crum III, Claire Diaz-Ortiz, Karen Dimmick, Kate Erickson, Dave M. Lukas, Caitlin Pyle, and Creek Stewart. You rock!

A big shout out to Chandler Bolt, Sean Sumner, and the Self-Publishing School Mastermind group. You supported me and encouraged me each step along the way.

I'm deeply grateful for all my friends, clients, podcast guests, mastermind colleagues and partners who support my business every day in little and big ways. You're my inspiration to create this book.

Thank you, Mom, for encouraging me to keep going no matter what, and to stay strong in the toughest times. I love you.

And, of course, a huge thanks to you, dear reader, for your trust and for your desire to make a difference in the world. You're magnificent.

Notes

1. Online Cambridge Dictionary: http://dictionary.cambridge.org/us/dictionary/english/influencer (accessed October 29, 2017)

2. "Decoy Video" on YouTube https://youtu.be/F-TyP-fYMDK8 (accessed October 29, 2017)

3. Small Business Trends Study https://smallbiztrends.com/2014/06/small-businesses-get-customers-through-word-of-mouth.html (accessed October 29, 2017)

4. Steve Jobs quote https://www.brainyquote.com/quotes/steve_jobs_416929?src=t_work_hard (accessed November 27, 2017)

5. Abraham Lincoln quote https://www.brainyquote.com/quotes/quotes/a/abrahamlin109275.html (accessed October 29, 2017)

6. Mahatma Gandhi quote https://www.goodreads.com/quotes/50584-your-beliefs-become-your-thoughts-your-thoughts-become-your-words (accessed November 27, 2017)

7. Dr. Wayne W. Dyer: *You'll See It When You Believe It*, Kindle edition, p.126 http://amzn.to/2gKlKyw

8. Steve Jobs quote http://www.goodreads.com/ quotes/629623-i-m-convinced-that-about-half-of-what-separates-the-successful (accessed October 29, 2017)

9. James Altucher blog http://www.jamesaltucher. com/2014/05/the-ultimate-guide-for-becoming-an-idea-machine/ (accessed October 29, 2017)

10. Unbounce website https://unbounce.com/conversion-glossary/definition/unique-value-proposition/ (accessed October 29, 2017)

11. Evan Carmichael, *Your One Word*, 10, Tarcher and Perigee, 2016, http://amzn.to/2qXEB0W

12. Mailchimp, "Average Email Campaign Stats of Mailchimp Customers by Industry" https://mailchimp. com/resources/research/email-marketing-benchmarks/ (accessed October 29, 2017)

13. Daily Mail, http://www.dailymail.co.uk/sciencetech/ article-2593459/Which-face-happily-disgusted-Scientists-discover-humans-21-different-facial-expressions.html (accessed October 29, 2017)

14. Misfit Entrepreneur Podcast "About Me" webpage http:// www.misfitentrepreneur.com/about.html (accessed October 29, 2017)

15. Podcasters Paradise https://www.cloriskylie.com/ podcastersparadise/

16. Quora https://www.quora.com/How-many-blogs-exist-in-the-world (accessed October 29, 2017)

17. Hubspot's Blog https://blog.hubspot.com/marketing/ blogging-time-benchmark (accessed October 29, 2017)

18. Alexa Traffic rank http://www.alexa.com/siteinfo (accessed August 22, 2017)

19. Jeff Walker, *Launch: An Internet Millionaire's Secret Formula to Sell Almost Anything Online, Build A Business You Love, and Live the Life of Your Dreams,* Morgan James Publishing, 61, http://amzn.to/2id1Rk9

20. Marianne Williamson quote https://www.brainyquote. com/quotes/marianne_williamson_635534?src=t_challenges (accessed December 13, 2017)

21. Leonardo da Vinci quote https://www.brainyquote.com/ quotes/leonardo_da_vinci_120052 (accessed December 13, 2017)

Cloris Kylie's Influencer Marketing Resources

Beyond Influencer Marketing **Book Bonuses ($197 value).** Ready-to-use templates to kickstart your influencer marketing campaign. www.beyondinfluencermarketing.com/bonuses

"Beyond Influencer Marketing" Podcast. Weekly chats with top entrepreneurs and case studies to build long-lasting connections with influential people. www.cloriskylie.com/podcast

Cloris Kylie's Personalized Client Attraction and Influencer Marketing Programs. To apply for a complimentary consultation with Cloris, visit: www.cloriskylie.com/consultation

"Beyond Influencer Marketing" Group Coaching Program. Step-by-step guidance to connect with people of influence to reach your ideal clients, grow your list, and boost your revenue. www.beyondinfluencermarketing.com/group

Cloris Kylie's Recommended Business Resources. Tools and programs to build authority, attract the right clients, and grow your magnificent business. www.cloriskylie.com/resources/

Sharing the Message

I'd love to have your help spreading the message.

If you've been inspired by *Beyond Influencer Marketing*, please pass it along or give it as a gift for another entrepreneur who might also benefit from this incredibly powerful way to build authority, grow your list, and boost revenue.

The recipients of your gift will remember you as the person who introduced them to this business philosophy, so you'll deepen your connections with them.

Also, I would be extremely grateful if you could leave a quick review on Amazon. Your reviews and recommendations to friends are essential for me to spread the message and help other entrepreneurs who are also eager to reveal their magnificence. Thank you in advance for your support!

Finally, get in touch! I can't wait to see and hear about your progress. I'm honored to play a part in your entrepreneurial journey.

About the Author

Cloris Kylie, marketing MBA and influencer marketing specialist, shows you how to create a strong marketing foundation and tap into connections with influencers to grow a magnificent business that thrives over the long term.

The author of the #1 bestselling book, *Beyond Influencer Marketing*, Cloris has grown a large network of influencers who have played an essential role in the growth of her coaching and consulting business..

The host of "Beyond Influencer Marketing Podcast" and "Magnificent Time for Entrepreneurs," she has interviewed bestselling authors and internationally-renowned entrepreneurs such as Chris Brogan, Dorie Clark, Dov Baron, Bob Burg, Neil Patel, Ryan Levesque, John Lee Dumas, Mel Abraham, and Serena, Saje, and Skye Dyer, the three daughters of Dr. Wayne W. Dyer.

Cloris has been featured on network television, dozens of virtual summits, and on top-ranked podcasts and YouTube shows, including the #1 podcast for entrepreneurs, Entrepreneurs On Fire.

Cloris's articles have been published on websites with millions of followers, such as TinyBuddha, MindBodyGreen, and Addicted2Success.

Cloris's unique background in industrial engineering and marketing allows her to design efficient and effective solutions for her clients, but Cloris knows you need more than tactics to succeed. That's why she also empowers you to, as she says, "Reveal your magnificence."

A lover of nature, Cloris enjoys hiking, biking, and photographing the spectacular birds of Southern New England, the place she calls home.

Find more resources to connect with influencers and attract the right clients at:

Website: www.ClorisKylie.com

Connect with Cloris on social media:

Facebook: www.facebook.com/ClorisKylie

Twitter: www.twitter.com/ClorisKylie

LinkedIn: www.linkedin.com/in/ClorisKylie/

BONUS: Free membership for readers of *Beyond Influencer Marketing* ($197 value)

Claim your free templates to kickstart your influencer marketing efforts and help you grow your magnificent business...

- Intro email formula to expand your network and get referrals

- Copy-and-paste templates:

  - Podcast pitch

  - TV appearance pitch

  - Guest-post pitch

And much more! Claim your book bonuses now:

www.beyondinfluencermarketing.com/bonuses